INFORMATION SECURITY

INFORMATION SECURITY

A MANAGER'S GUIDE TO THWARTING DATA THIEVES AND HACKERS

Philip Alexander

PSI Business Security
W. Timothy Coombs, Series Editor

PRAEGER SECURITY INTERNATIONAL
Westport, Connecticut • London

Library of Congress Cataloging-in-Publication Data

Information security: a manager's guide to thwarting data thieves and hackers /
  Philip Alexander.
    p. cm. — (PSI business security)
    Includes bibliographical references and index.
    ISBN-13: 978-0-313-34558-6 (alk. paper)
1. Business enterprises—Computer networks—Security measures. 2. Information
technology—Security measures. 3. Computer security. 4. Data protection. I. Title.
HF5548.37.A44 2008
005.8—dc22   2007043997

British Library Cataloguing in Publication Data is available.

Library of Congress Catalog Card Number: 2007043997
ISBN-13: 978-0-313-34558-6

First published in 2008

Praeger Security International, 88 Post Road West, Westport, CT 06881
An imprint of Greenwood Publishing Group, Inc.
www.praeger.com

Printed in the United States of America

∞

The paper used in this book complies with the
Permanent Paper Standard issued by the National
Information Standards Organization (Z39.48–1984).

10 9 8 7 6 5 4 3 2 1

CONTENTS

Preface: The Heartbreak of Data Loss   vii

Acknowledgments   ix

1. Computer Use and Data Security Policies and Standards   1

2. Network/DMZ Design   20

3. Defense in Depth   30

4. Authentication and Authorization   51

5. Security and the Mobile Employee   64

6. Business Continuity Planning   71

7. Hackers, Snoops, and Viruses   82

8. Personnel Issues and Hiring Practices   93

9. Contractual Considerations   115

10. Data Privacy Laws   121

11. Overseas Outsourcing   133

Appendix A: The Trusted Computer System Evaluation Criteria   141
        (TCSEC)

Appendix B: Rainbow Series   145

Appendix C: The International Organization for Standardization   149
        (ISO)

Glossary   161

Index   173

PREFACE: THE HEARTBREAK OF DATA LOSS

What would be the impact if your company lost critical data? The answer to that question varies depending on the nature of the data itself. Some data is regulated by the government. If that data is compromised as a result of a security breach, your company could be in violation of a number of laws and regulations. Data loss could also mean that your company couldn't make accurate and timely financial reports or even respond to a judge's subpoena. And if the data is about your company's newest wonder drug or next generation electronic gadget, losing that information or letting it fall into the wrong hands could cost millions.

Data loss can have serious repercussions.

A couple of years back at a computer security symposium, attendees were asked what the worst type of data loss would be. The majority responded with the conventional wisdom—it would be a total loss of all the information on a major system such as a large database or other major system of record. That's the wrong answer. Most companies perform regular backups, and this type of catastrophic data loss would be easy to spot and recover from the backups. A more damaging situation would be a series of small, hard-to-notice changes that over time invalidated or compromised the data. Since it would be hard to detect, your backups would be tainted as well, thus making recovery much more difficult. Another data risk would be to lose information bit by bit, the work of an insider adept at covering his tracks while bleeding the company dry. Data exposure is just as serious a risk as data loss.

Moreover, depending on the nature of the information, and the number of records, the fines associated with a data breach could run into millions of dollars. There are laws that hold people criminally liable for certain types of data loss, some of which are felonies. Note that I'm not talking about hackers, but rather the executives who failed to adequately protect the data itself.

This book focuses on the factors involved in protecting your company's data, as well as its computing resources. As you'll see, I take what is known as the C-I-A approach, which stands for Confidentiality, Integrity, and Availability. In other words, safeguarding your company's data is not just limited to warding off the intentional misdeeds of hackers.

This book is all about knowing what your risks are when it comes to information security, and what solutions are available to manage the risks. I take a pragmatic approach, keeping an eye on the bottom line. I look at the real benefits of solutions that are available today, what they can do, and what they can't.

I also clear up some common misconceptions. For example, there are no silver bullets that will solve all your problems at once. If somebody is telling you otherwise, he or she is probably a salesperson whose knowledge is limited to what they've read in their product's marketing brochure.

This book takes an international approach, as many companies now have a presence in several countries, such as the United States, the European Union, India, and elsewhere. And I cover a broad spectrum of issues that will arm you with the knowledge to understand the challenges faced in trying to both manage and secure the data in your company's computer network as well as the data entrusted to third parties at home and abroad.

In short, this book will make you better prepared to meet the challenges of keeping information safe and secure head on.

Note: This book contains an extensive glossary. If you run across a word or concept you don't know, chances are that I have defined it in the glossary. It will also help to befriend an articulate IT person in your company. Since this book is not designed to explain concepts or procedures in great depth, that IT person can help you understand how these ideas play out in the real world.

We have a lot to cover; let's get started.

ACKNOWLEDGMENTS

If there's anything that I've learned from becoming an author, it is that writing a book is not an individual effort. Help and inspiration comes from many sources, and I'd like to take this opportunity to recognize a few of the people who have been invaluable in the making of this book.

First off, I'd like to thank Jillian Testa. The term "genius" is tossed around far too easily these days. However, Jillian is truly a singularly brilliant woman. As a smart man who's by no means a genius, I reached out to Jillian, who helped me in editing many of my chapters. Thanks, Jillian, I really appreciate your help.

I'd also like to extend a measure of gratitude to my editor Jeff Olson. While I have over 20 years of experience in the IT field, I am not quite as tenured as a published author. This is in fact my second book. Jeff was more than patient in working with the many edits that were required throughout the book in order to bring it to its current level of polish. Thanks, Jeff.

I also want to recognize Myrna Pfeifer. My Aunt Myrna has been very supportive over the past year as I've been writing this book. Of course, my Aunt Myrna has always supported me throughout my entire life. She's a very special person who possesses a wisdom that I've come to appreciate all the more over the years. You're the best, Aunt Myrna.

Finally, and most importantly, I want to thank my wife Cency and our two sons Freddy and Danny. Writing a book takes countless hours of research and typing. It takes time away from the family, which is no small cost. Through it all, they've been very patient and understanding.

CHAPTER 1

COMPUTER USE AND DATA SECURITY POLICIES AND STANDARDS

All companies have policies. Policies cover a wide range of issues, from hiring to firing and from compensation scales to sick leave and vacation time. In the areas of computer usage and data security, policies are needed to provide direction for safeguarding your company's sensitive information, whether it's non-public customer information such as a person's Social Security number or prerelease information about your company's newest invention. Comprehensive security policies can also help to protect your company from fraud and embezzlement. And depending on the industry you're in and the country where your company is located, there are any number of laws and regulations your company will have to follow, requiring yet more policies.

Who should have computer usage and data security policies and standards? Every organization that handles sensitive data, or that has employees using the company's computer resources. While this advice may be more obvious for the government, the financial sector, health care, and the credit card industry, it applies to every business, no matter how small.

For example, without a computer-usage policy, your company may be held financially liable if one of your employees hacks into another company's systems from your network. Then there are situations such as harassing e-mails, visiting inappropriate Web sites (pornography, gambling, etc.), and employees stealing software and loading it on their work computers. Without computer-use policies specifically banning these types of activities, your company could be held civilly—and in some cases criminally—liable for these actions.

Let's look first at some of the areas that require policies and standards, and then how to create them.

UNAUTHORIZED SOFTWARE

It's against the law to steal software. But loading unapproved applications into your computer system can carry risks beyond the possibility of software piracy. Unauthorized programs can also infect your company's network with a virus, Trojan horse, or other type of malware. I generally recommend that companies specifically forbid employees from loading unapproved software on company-provided workstations or laptops. (But you needn't be too stringent. For example, I have loaded a jpeg picture of my two sons on my work computer and use it as my desktop background. While there's a risk in doing that, you don't want to be so Draconian that the security benefits are outweighed by the negative impact to your employees.)

Even if the unapproved software doesn't have a virus, it can be incompatible with your company's computer systems. It is a sound technical practice therefore to require that, before new software is loaded onto a production system, it go through a technical review to ensure it's compatible with your company's systems.

But don't review it on your "production"—computer systems that house your company's data or that are used to run normal business functions. Instead, have a system used specifically for both the development and testing of new applications or processes. Having a segregated "development environment" like this allows you to conduct research without undue risk.

Software that has not been through a rigorous technical review, recreational or not, may cause systems to crash. What is the cost to your company of system down time? What is the cost to dispatch a computer support engineer to fix a system outage caused by unauthorized software?

I remember being asked to look at an end-user's workstation that had run out of hard drive space. What I found was that over two-thirds of the computer's hard-drive space was taken up by the end-user's virtual golf games. Now, I don't have anything against the game of golf—aside from my wicked slice—but games are not a good use of work computer's disk space. You also have to wonder how much time this person spent playing golf games rather than performing his job.

WEB MAIL SERVICES

Web mail services such as Yahoo, Hotmail, MSN, etc., are free for anyone with Internet access. These and other free e-mail services like them are a great way for people to communicate with each other. Nonetheless, I strongly recommend that companies prohibit employees from accessing Web e-mail accounts from work computers. Such accounts are not well monitored; people are free to send any kind of content they want. While some Web e-mail providers do perform virus checking of e-mails, I still would not permit them to be used on work computers. Having anti-virus software, and keeping the definition files current, are two different things.

The larger concern is that most Web e-mail services don't filter for what many would consider inappropriate content. Depending on the nature of the material, having it appear on a work computer's monitor could be construed as sexual harassment. I enjoy a good e-mail joke as much as the next person, but not from my work computer. In today's world, what might be funny to one person could very well be offensive to another, resulting in a complaint to your human resources department—or the Equal Opportunity Employment Commission.

Our work e-mails label us as employees, or at least affiliates, of the companies we work for. Consider what the public relations effect would be if the press discovered that employees of your company were sending and receiving off-color e-mails. Perhaps even more embarrassing would be questionable communications from a government agency. Tax payers might not appreciate seeing crude joke e-mails being sent around by "employee@publicsectorjob.gov."

E-MAIL/INTERNET MONITORING

Does your company reserve the right to read employee e-mails? Does your company reserve the right to inspect e-mail messages that are being sent to outside addresses, and to block them if necessary? If not, start. And be sure to mention these rights in your internal policies. It also helps employees, particularly new hires, to know your expectations up front regarding the computer assets that they use as part of their duties. While some consider such policies an invasion of privacy, companies have a vested interest in monitoring what their employees are doing on company computers. Many e-mail servers on the market today will store e-mails that are sent both to and from employees' accounts. This allows employers to read e-mails as needed in the event of a suspected breach of policy. There are also software packages on the market today that allow for the real-time inspection of the content of e-mail.

Let's look at some sample e-mails, sent from company servers, that an employer would want to know about:

- E-mail to stock broker: "I just heard that our new experimental cancer drug won't be approved by the Food and Drug Administration. Quick—sell all my shares!"

- E-mail to the local newspaper: "Hey Bob, we just got hacked again. These guys are too cheap to encrypt data. This is the third time in two years we've been compromised. They got millions of our customer records. It's really going to hit the fan now!"
- E-mail to fellow male coworker: "Quick, check out what Carol is wearing today. Man is she hot!"

The three scenarios above could have a serious impact on a company. With a computer usage policy that clearly advises your employees that any e-mails sent from their work computers are subject to search, your company could respond appropriately. Moreover, the first two e-mails actually suggest the need to invest in technologies capable of stopping e-mails before they leave your company. There are solutions available that can inspect the content of outgoing e-mails, including instant messages, and permit companies to stop this type of information from leaving the network. As for the third scenario, deal with it by having a policy that prohibits sexual harassment in addition to a policy that lets employees know that the company can read employee e-mails sent from, or received on, work computers.

NON-DISCLOSURE AND NON-COMPETE AGREEMENTS

Aside from the use of company equipment, policies need to cover how employees use the information they acquire as part of their job. Non-disclosure policies can protect your company from employees sharing sensitive data with your competitors. Non-compete clauses for employees leaving the company are also common. They generally forbid an employee from working for a competitor in the same industry for a defined period of time. Even beyond the finite time period generally included in a non-compete clause, if your company is involved in research and development, marketing, or has client lists, you're going to want to forbid any former employees from using such information for a time period beyond its usefulness.

INTELLECTUAL PROPERTY

Many companies have policies stating that any intellectual property created or research conducted as part of an employee's employment is generally considered to be the property of the company. This type of policy keeps an employee from using their job as a personal research laboratory. Some companies, however, encourage their employees to conduct research and get published. An obvious example would be colleges and universities. It's wise, therefore, to create some contractual/policy language describing what is appropriate, and who owns the rights, either in whole or part, to the publication or invention so there are no misunderstandings. You may even want to be consulted first before such works are released. You have a vested interest in ensuring that the work doesn't disclose any sensitive information, or reflect poorly on your company.

UNETHICAL AND ILLEGAL BEHAVIOR

Companies should provide employees with documented procedures on how to report what they believe to be illegal or unethical behavior. Commonly referred to as a whistleblower policy, employees need to know that they can report such behavior without fear of repercussions. Your employees need to know that such complaints will be investigated, and that the source of the tip will remain anonymous. It is not uncommon for such circumstances to involve an employee's co-worker or manager. A whistleblower policy can be a very powerful tool for uncovering acts of unethical behavior. It can also serve to demonstrate that the company itself has high ethical standards by encouraging this type of internal policing.

As important as these types of policies are for your internal employees, they are perhaps even more important for your contractors and vendors. This is because, while companies will give both contractors and vendors access to data equivalent to that of their own employees, they often do not submit them to the same level of oversight in areas such as background checks and data use policies. A frequently quoted statistic in the field is that 80 percent of data theft is internal. Even so, not all internal theft is due to employees. Contractors and vendors that are given internal access to systems steal data as well. Contractual issues specific to relations with contractors and vendors are discussed more in depth in Chapter 9.

It makes sense that most data theft would be internal since the perpetrators are already on the inside and don't have to bypass a company's perimeter security measures. The statistic actually makes a strong argument for implementing security controls beyond the normal perimeter measures of firewalls and intrusion detection sensors. It also demonstrates why many companies should routinely scan their end-users' systems to, among other reasons, check for suspicious activities.

JOB SHARING AND JOB ROTATION

An effective method to reduce internal data theft and fraud is to have policies that require both job sharing and job rotation, at least among certain positions or job categories. Job sharing entails having a certain set of responsibilities shared among two or more individuals. If you're the only person who knows how a certain activity is done, it makes it all the easier to exploit that monopoly of knowledge for fraudulent purposes.

Sharing job functions among a few people makes committing fraud much more difficult. It actually forces the would-be fraudster to engage in collusion as well. She would have to discuss her illegal plans with the other employee, hoping that person would either participate or at a minimum not turn her in. Having to involve another person can be an effective deterrent in itself. There is also an added benefit to having more than one person know how to perform a business task. It makes coverage easier for vacation and sick days, and is less likely to cause an issue if somebody either leaves the company or transfers to another position.

Job rotation entails having people perform a certain job function for a fixed period of time, and then moving them to something else. This has similar benefits to job sharing, because it also reduces fraud and provides cross-training.

Having a policy for separation of duties is another effective way to deter fraud. For example, your company should have a policy that forbids developers who write application code from having access to the application once it's loaded on production systems. Allowing developers to have access to the code that they write once it's on a production system would enable them to make use of any "back doors" they may have written into the code. Access to the software in production allows the use of the back door to bypass system security and commit fraud. Further, require software developers to document their work fully. This will make troubleshooting easier for the engineers who provide production support.

Such separation of duties is an effective deterrent to fraud. Many developers also have a bad habit of developing directly on production systems. Placing untested software on a production system can have unknown results. Nobody can know the effect that new lines of software code, or any untested application, will have on a company's systems without fully testing it first. This type of activity can cause serious availability issues with your production systems. Requiring developers to work solely in a development environment eliminates that risk.

REVIEW RAW SOURCE CODE

For companies that deal in sensitive information, I recommend having a policy that requires a security review of the raw source code before installing it on your production systems. This is particularly true when the data will be accessible over the Internet. Due to the massive storage capacity of today's computers, it is not uncommon for applications to contain hundreds of thousands—or even millions—of lines of code. Having a qualified engineer review the raw source code for any exploits, and subsequently requiring that they be fixed prior to going into production, can plug huge security holes. (Exploits in computer code are weaknesses that a hacker can take advantage of to either steal data or cause a system outage.) Whether intentional or strictly a matter of poor coding practices, it is very common for applications to contain security holes that a hacker can exploit to gain unauthorized access to your company's systems and data.

Here again, I recommend a sense of proportionality. Depending on the particular environment, it is not good business practice to require that all possible security holes, no matter the severity, be patched prior to allowing software to be loaded on your company's systems. Concentrate on the more serious security issues. The focus of this book is not an in-depth review of the various vulnerabilities found in application source code today. However, as application security is so critical in protecting a company's electronic data, it's something you need to know about. Go to http://vulncat.fortifysoftware.com for a good overview of a wide range of exploits found in propriety software being used today. While this Web site is an excellent guide, it is also necessary to work with subject matter experts on this very technical aspect of data security.

CHANGES TO PRODUCTION SYSTEMS

I recommend that companies have a mature, well-documented policy regarding changes being made to production systems. Production systems are those that are used to run your company, or that store data needed by those systems. Since computer networks will vary so much from company to company, it's also worth discussing which systems are considered "non-production" systems. Non-production systems are generally used for the development and testing of new software, patches, or business processes. Such systems need to be separate from production systems in order to minimize the risks of accidentally impacting them and consequently disrupting your key business processes.

Another way to protect production systems is to create what's called a MAC ("Moves—Adds—Changes") review policy prior to allowing changes to go into a production environment. The policy should require that the proposed change be specifically documented. Whether it's a software upgrade, adding a new server, or making changes to firewall rules, the scope should be clearly and completely documented. Identify any affected systems, in addition to stakeholders of the systems so they can be made aware of the potential risks. Include a back-out strategy in case the implementation is not successful. Most companies also have "change windows," generally after normal business hours, to minimize the impact to both customers and employees.

Policies that temporarily block making any changes to a network, also known as network freezes, are recommended for companies that have regular critical reporting periods, such as end of the month or end of the year tax reporting. You don't want to risk a network outage during such critical time frames. An actual change control form requiring all relevant information is a good way to ensure compliance. Software packages such as Remedy and Heat have fairly comprehensive change control forms. With a certain amount of customization, they could be made to fit the needs of a wide range of companies. It is possible to configure such systems to send out e-mails automatically, notifying stakeholders that they have a change to review and approve as appropriate. This type of procedure is even more critical when a change requires the review from a security, legal, or compliance perspective. While a mature change control policy is very important, it needs to be flexible enough to allow for emergency changes in the event of a system outage. You do not want your company's change-control policy to cause extensive down time of critical systems because of all the required paperwork.

COMPANY CREDIT CARDS AND EXPENSE ACCOUNTS

Many organizations also provide certain employees with company credit cards or some kind of expense account to cover business-related costs. This is particularly true with positions that entail a significant amount of traveling. From a fraud-reduction perspective, no person should be allowed to approve their own business expenses. Your company should also have policies that specify spending limits on air fare, hotels, and meals. In addition, they should detail what types of entertainment expenses are permissible. For example, I believe that allowing managers to take their teams out to lunch on occasion provides a good atmosphere in which to build team spirit, and it can be a real morale booster. That said, it is not a good business practice to let your employees dine out every day and charge it on their company credit cards.

PREFERRED VENDORS AND APPROVED EQUIPMENT LISTS

It is not uncommon for companies to have a preferred vendors list. Approved vendors are those that provide your company with special pricing for their products based on a negotiated contract. Requiring employees to use only approved vendors can save your company money in other ways as well. Purchasing products and services from a defined list of vendors allows companies to secure preferred pricing. A list of vendors approved at the corporate level will also deter employees and managers from trying to conduct business with vendors in which they have a material interest. This type of conflict of interest can result in improper purchasing decisions and compromise a company's normal oversight of vendors.

In addition to requiring employees to work from an approved vendors list, you should consider mandating an approved equipment list as well.

A clearly defined and limited set of hardware and software is not only less expensive, it is also easier to support and secure. For example, if employees need to have printers either at work or at their home office, having them choose from a short list of printers can save money. It also prevents an employee from purchasing a multi-function printer and hooking up the fax modem. If the faxing capability is not needed, don't assume the risk of having a printer attached to both your network and the telephone line. Aside from the security implications, there are also interoperability considerations when choosing hardware components. It is much easier to deploy workstations and laptops when you can load the software from a pre-determined and centrally managed configuration. This is also known as a master image file. If you are working from a limited list of peripheral hardware components, it makes building such an image file that much easier.

Certain hardware peripherals carry a lot of risk. You can hook up thumb drives, for example, to a computer's USB port and copy large amounts of data. The capacity of thumb drives today are measured in gigabytes, and will certainly only get larger with time. In addition, most MP3 music players can also store other types of data aside from audio files. Similar to thumb drives, they plug into USB ports and can copy and store vast amounts of data. I am not suggesting that companies forbid employees from listening to music. However, a radio with a CD player and a set of headphones is less of a risk to your network then an MP3 player. For the MP3 zealots out there, many portable CD players can also play music files that are in the MP3 format. You can listen to your downloaded music without bringing a tiny multi-gigabyte storage device into work.

If your company allows the use of PDAs, as with any other type of hardware peripheral, you should have policies in place mandating that only approved PDAs are to be used. Again, it is too hard to support or secure all of the different types of PDAs available in the market today. Beyond the security implications, there is also the possibility that certain hardware components might not be compatible with each other. Requiring employees to work off of an approved list avoids those types of issues.

COPYING DATA

Do you know how many copies of sensitive data are floating around on floppy disks, CDs, or thumb drives within your company? For most companies the answer is no, which in itself can present a risk. A way to begin to address this issue is to create a policy prohibiting copying data to CD or any other type of external storage device drive, including external hard drives. Some companies have taken to purchasing workstations that do not contain either "floppy" drives or CD-ROM drives. It is also possible to disable a computer's USB ports. Having such restrictions as part of your standard system builds will help to mitigate risk.

WIRELESS ROUTERS

It is common for employees working out of their homes to use wireless routers. This technology permits them to work from any room in the house—or even in the backyard! Unfortunately, most end-users lack the technical expertise to properly secure their wireless networks, and as a result, they are introducing risk into the company network. A hacker can steal sensitive data from a computer if it is attached to a wireless network that is not properly secured.

Since you probably don't have the resources to send engineers out to employees' homes to make sure their wireless networks are properly secured and that patches and anti-virus files are being properly updated, restrict employees from using their home wireless network for work purposes. This can be achieved at a technical level by either not installing a wireless network card, or disabling wireless networking as part of your company's standard laptop configuration.

SECURING LAPTOPS

Laptops themselves create some interesting security issues, whether or not they are configured to use wireless. Many cases of data theft exist that took no more ingenuity than merely stealing a laptop. I recommend having a policy that requires hard drive encryption for the protection of all laptops to help prevent unauthorized access to the data if they are stolen.

Of course, it is better to try and keep the laptop from being stolen in the first place. While I am at work, for example, I secure my laptop to my desk with a cable lock. Sure, it is possible to cut a cable lock, but it makes the task that much more difficult for the would-be thief. While I do have hard-drive encryption on my laptop, I would just as soon not have to spend the money to purchase another one.

If any data is stored locally on the laptop, it will be lost if the laptop is stolen. In most instances, the data on laptops is not backed up as regularly as data on servers. In the name of both data confidentiality and availability, I recommend having data stored on servers that users access via laptops, rather than right on the laptop itself.

NEEDED: EFFECTIVE, COMPREHENSIVE POLICIES

All of the issues that I've outlined require effective and comprehensive policies. Data security is such a new field that most people know little more than the absolute basics. Plug in a firewall, and those same people will believe that their network is hack-proof. Comprehensive security policies are required not only to protect your company's assets, but to also help raise the level of awareness of your employees. It is important, then, to include a section in each policy explaining its rationale. This is not to serve as a justification for the respective security policies, but the reality is that people are more likely to comply with a given policy if they can understand its value. Even very technical people will often look at security policies with a certain degree of skepticism. Most computer users, engineers or not, are focused on functionality, and see security policies as something that slows them up and costs them money.

This becomes even more of an issue when that computer user also happens to be a manager or an executive. While politics is a reality that can not easily be dismissed, policies that do not comply with government regulations or safe computing practices only serve to put a company at risk.

Writing effective policies also takes highly skilled professionals. Some companies hire outside consultants to write effective policies, while others rely on in-house talent—HR people or IT managers skilled in writing.

Any of the big consulting firms can help write policies. In any case, numerous organizations can assist companies in the creation of security policies. Such firms will generally recommend policies that meet industry best practices. The challenge is making the policies work within the internal organizational culture that makes each company unique. For that reason, internal security professionals are an important part of any company. Outside consulting firms should augment a company's security staff, and not replace it.

POLICY CONSIDERATIONS

When going through the process of either writing policies or making changes to existing policies, there are several things that should be considered. As I have mentioned earlier, your company's policies need to be compliant with any laws that apply to the industry you are in, the nature of the data that is involved, and, of course, the country or countries you are operating in. Policies by their nature are high level, and serve as a guide. Control standards, baselines, and procedures provide increasingly more specific levels of information on how to comply with the higher-level policies. Policies need to be attainable, and they should take into account issues such as cost and level of effort, in addition to other mitigating controls.

Say you're considering a policy that dictates that all non-public customer information has to be encrypted while stored on systems, or while in transit, within your company. Yet many older legacy systems exist that do not have proven encryption solutions available. A good example of such a legacy system would be mainframes. Having older systems is a good argument for comprehensive security controls to protect sensitive data when encryption might not be feasible. Is your company prepared to update every system and application that doesn't have a solution to encrypt the data that's stored on them? For that matter, does your company have the technical wherewithal to encrypt all sensitive data while in transit? While there are many firewalls and routers that can encrypt data, the added traffic load would need to be accounted for when determining network usage levels. A company that is going to encrypt data needs to develop a strategy for the protection of the encryption keys. Consider what the impact would be if your company lost its encryption keys, and therefore could not access the sensitive data.

Passwords and other authentication credentials are often considered very sensitive, and rightfully so. However, if a password only grants access to a single system with relatively non-sensitive data, should it be treated the same way as a password that gives access to a company's master system of record containing hundreds of millions of sensitive customer files? I pose this question to illustrate the need to look at the whole picture when making policy, as well as implementing and inter-preting that policy. Companies need to consider that nature of the access that a given password provides. If it provides view-only access to a system that contains non-sensitive data, then safeguarding the password becomes less of a security issue.

An argument for not having comprehensive data security policies is that your company will not be able to comply with all of them all of the time. The truth is that most companies are out of compliance to varying degrees on a regular basis. Security policies serve as a guide, and they provide executives with an idea of the risks of non-compliance. They need to be written with an eye toward regulatory compliance and not adopted only if easily attainable. When making security policy and assessing the risks of non-compliance with a given policy, a comprehensive view is needed.

For example, the risk of a data compromise may be offset to a certain degree by other compensating controls. Many large companies have data centers with multiple levels of both physical and logical controls to protect the systems. Does this eliminate the need for encryption? No. It simply means that a server in a data center is better protected than one in an open-cube environment in an administrative building. This is important to illustrate the need to take a big-picture approach when writing as well as enforcing data security policies. You should take other compensating controls, in this example the protective physical controls of placing a server in a data center, into account when creating a policy requiring encryption for all sensitive data. While encryption is a powerful tool to help maintain the confidentiality of data, it is not the end-all to data protection. Encryption is designed to protect the confidentiality of data from unauthorized users. It offers little protection if the system itself is compromised. Therefore, companies need to take a comprehensive approach to data security. This concept is also known as defense in depth, something covered in detail in Chapter 3. Policies to safeguard data that take a well thought out and multilayered approach are better able to help ensure a comprehensive protective posture.

Take care not to write policies that contain obvious technical inaccuracies. Such inaccuracies can actually put sensitive data at risk, may waste limited security resources, and certainly will not pass the scrutiny of an audit. As an example, I was actually told during a presentation of a vendor's risk assessment tool that one of the risks of sensitive data being unencrypted on back-up tapes was that the actual tapes could be physically damaged in the event of either a car accident or a plane crash. Now, I do agree that storing sensitive data on tape unencrypted does present a risk. However, in this case the presenter was stating that the lack of encryption made the tape more susceptible to physical damage in the event of a car crash. The individual was confusing a logical control with a physical threat. When I brought this up, another presenter tried to explain to me how the lack of encryption actually increased the likelihood of physical damage to the tape itself—another absurdity.

The lesson here is to know who is drafting your company's data policies. Watch out for obvious lack of subject matter expertise, as was demonstrated by this type of glaring error. Encryption wouldn't save data on tapes in the event of a fire. A more appropriate control for that particular risk would be placing the backup tapes inside a fireproof safe.

INDUSTRY STANDARDS

Industry sources like trade or professional associations publish sample standards and guidelines. They provide very useful information that many companies use as a guide when developing their own internal policies. This is particularly helpful since many auditors also use these standards when reviewing a company's security posture. If you use them to help create comprehensive security policies, remember that such guidelines are not a substitute for seasoned professionals. Nonetheless, some industry sources can be quite useful, and in some cases are recognized standards that regulators and auditors work from.

The International Organization for Standardization, for example, publishes the well known ISO standards. The ISO 17799 is a good standard that takes a comprehensive look at the protection of data. It is used here in the United States, as well as the European Union, India and more.

As of 2007, the ISO 17799/27002—27001 is the most current iteration of the standard. The Web site is www.iso.org. The new international version of the standard clarifies and strengthens the requirements of the original British standard, and includes changes to the following areas:

- risk assessment,
- contractual obligations,
- scope,
- management decisions, and
- measuring the effectiveness of selected controls.

NIST, the National Institute for Standards and Technology (www.nist.gov), has a wealth of information. Many of the data breach disclosure laws in the United States require that a company show due diligence in protecting sensitive data. Following the guidelines as outlined by NIST would go a long way toward proving such due diligence. An example would be using encryption algorithms recommended by NIST to protect your company's sensitive information. NIST can also serve as a guide to technical best practices. For example, NIST certifies encryption algorithms based on how hard they are to break. Once an algorithm has been broken, NIST will decertify it. Companies should mandate that a NIST certified encryption algorithm protect their sensitive data. As of this writing, 3-DES and AES-256 are the two NIST certified encryption algorithms. Of the two, AES-256 is the stronger algorithm.

There's also the Federal Financial Institutions Examination Council (FFIEC) at www.ffiec.gov. The FFIEC is a formal interagency organization that is empowered to prescribe a set of common principles, standards, and report forms for the federal examination of financial institutions doing business within the United States by the Board of Governors of the Federal Reserve System, the Federal Deposit Insurance Corporation, the Office of the Comptroller of the Currency, the National Credit Unit Administration, and the Office of Thrift Supervision. For the payment card industry there's the PCI Security Standards Council, www.pcisecuritystandards.org.

These agencies provide guidance to the financial sector, and in the case of PCI Security Standards, focus on that particular aspect of the sector. You do not have to start from scratch; there is plenty of information to serve as a guide in writing data security policies.

The health care field has its own set of data privacy laws. The Health Insurance Portability and Accountability Act of 1996, HIPAA, is the main privacy law for health care and related industries in the United States. If you're in the health care field or have questions about the rules surrounding the protection of medical information you may have stored on your company's systems, I would recommend visiting www.hipaa.org.

Note: Most companies are not aware of the fact that HIPAA regulations may apply to them even if they are not the health care industry. If your company provides health insurance for its employees and maintains medical records (as part of oversight or in order to provide some statistics for measuring cost increases), then you need to understand HIPAA.

The Bank for International Settlements, Basel, (www.bis.org) is an excellent international resource for financial institutions. The Basel II framework provides a more comprehensive measure and minimum standards for capital adequacy that national supervisory authorities are now working to implement through domestic rule-making and adoption procedures. The Basel II framework seeks to improve on the existing rules by aligning regulatory capital requirements more closely to the underlying risks financial institutions are facing. The intention of the Basel II framework is to promote a forward-looking approach to capital supervision, one that encourages financial institutions to identify the risks they may face, today and in the future, as well as to develop or improve their ability to manage those risks.

In the United Kingdom, there's the Information Commissioner's Office, www.ico.gov.uk. The ICO is an independent public body set up to both promote access to official information and protect personal information by promoting good practice, ruling on eligible complaints, providing information to individuals and organizations, and taking appropriate action when the law is broken.

All of the resources that I've just listed vary to a certain degree as they target specific industries, specific countries, or specific issues concerning data security.

Another resource used in England, France, the Netherlands, and Germany, is the Information Technology Security Evaluation Criteria, or ITSEC (www.iwar.org.uk/comsec/resources/standards/itsec.htm). The ITSEC is a structured set of criteria for evaluating computer security within products and systems. The product or system being evaluated, called the *target of evaluation*, is subjected to a detailed examination of its security features, culminating in comprehensive and informed functional and penetration testing.

In the United States, the Trusted Computer System Evaluation Criteria, or TCSEC (www.boran.com/security/tcsec.html), is the answer to ITSEC. The TCSEC is a U.S. Department of Defense standard that sets basic requirements for assessing the effectiveness of computer security controls built into a computer system. The TCSEC is used to evaluate, classify, and select computer systems being considered for the processing, storage, and retrieval of sensitive or classified information. The TCSEC uses what is known as the Orange Book. The Orange Book is actually the unofficial name for the Trusted Computer System Evaluation Criteria (TCSEC).

The TCSEC Standard, or Orange Book, which is fully outlined in Appendix A, serves the following purposes:

1. Provides product manufacturers with a standard of security features to build into their products.
2. Provides Department of Defense components with a metric to evaluate how much trust can be placed in an automated information system for secure processing of classified or other sensitive data.
3. Provides a basis for specifying security requirements in acquisition specifications.

This list is by no means comprehensive, but the respective agencies and organizations do provide excellent information. In most cases, they are the standards that auditors are looking for and are what the respective industries are driving toward. No company's published guidelines, no matter how informative, are a substitute for highly skilled professionals in their respective fields. To be blunt, a business manager is not the right person to be creating security policies.

HOW TO COMPLY

Companies should provide guidance on how to comply with their policies and standards. For example, you should have a set of standard procedures for the configuration of the various type of computer operating systems currently deployed within your company. As the next-generation operating system comes to market, you will need to have procedures for how to configure it when it is deployed within your company's network. It is not possible to follow a set of nonexistent system configuration standards. In the absence of such standards, engineers building such systems will configure them based on their own opinion of what is best. This will effectively drive configuration standards from being a company standard to being an engineer's opinion. Large companies could end up with subtle variances in systems installed throughout the network. Such variances can be not only a security risk, but can also cause availability concerns. Patches and other software upgrades that worked fine on one system could cause another one to crash.

SELF-ASSESSMENTS

Depending on the type of industry you are in, you may actually be required to perform self-assessments of your organization's practices against your documented policies. This includes financial institutions as well as the payment card industry. Whether required or not, it's a good idea to perform self-assessments. Generally speaking, auditors will want to see that both your policies as well as your assessments are accurate, consistent, and repeatable. Self-assessment will also let you know where your company is out of compliance with its own policies. This will empower you to direct the necessary resources to work towards compliance in the areas of the greatest concern. Outside regulators are generally more understanding if a company can demonstrate that they are cognizant of where they are out of compliance, and are working to address it.

POLITICS AND POLICIES

Groups within your organization that are chartered with tasks such as conducting audits, creating data handling policy, and performing risk assessments need to operate as free from internal political pressures as possible. While a certain amount of oversight is always appropriate, be careful not to place these groups too low within the company hierarchy. This will put pressure on them to bend to the will of management rather than operate in an open and objective manner. A good rule of thumb is to have them report to either a chief auditor or a chief security officer. It is hard enough performing these types of oversight functions within your own company without compounding it with undue political pressures. Also bear in mind that an accurate security assessment or audit will identify the existence of compliance concerns. This will allow executives to decide on the appropriate course of action to remedy such issues.

Remember that risk is a part of doing business. Executives within any given organization routinely make decisions on all types of risk based on their experience and the information they have on a given situation. This is why having the best people in their respective fields is so critical. Presenting executives with the most accurate and comprehensive set of facts possible will empower them to make better decisions. The risks are out there; that's a constant. The variable is how accurately the risks are explained to the executives who may be legally bound to accept them whether they are fully informed or not. Bear in mind that sometimes the greatest risk can be missing out on a business opportunity. Appropriate levels of executive management need to be empowered to accept the risk of being out of compliance with a given policy. In such situations, it is common to develop an action plan, sometimes called a contingency, requiring the identified policy violation to be fixed within a defined period of time.

ASSESSING AND MEASURING RISK

An accurate security assessment needs to list three facets of risk. The three facets are: initial, mitigated, and residual. The following example illustrates the differences between the three terms. If sensitive data is unencrypted, the initial risk is that the data is compromised in the event of a breach. Depending on the nature of the data, such a compromise could require a company to disclose the breach to any affected customers, which can be very costly. Factors that mitigate the risk of compromised data include the server being in a data center and having strong authentication controls. In other words, mitigating controls lower the probability of a breach occurring. If at some point the data was encrypted, that would eliminate the risk of the data being unencrypted, which would be noted as the residual risk rating. So the residual risk is that what remains after security measures have been utilized. It's important to bear in mind that there is no such thing as the total absence of risk. The goal of a comprehensive security posture is to lower the residual or remaining risk to a level that is acceptable by management.

It is generally accepted in most cases that the risk lies with the data. The more sensitive the data, the greater the risk to an organization if the data is either lost or hacked. It would make sense, then, to focus your company's energies on protecting sensitive data, rather than all data. That's why you need to have clear policies that require the classification of the different types of data your company may have at any given time. I also recommend having no less than four levels of data classification to provide sufficient distinctions between the various types of information. An example would be: *public, internal use, confidential*, and *restricted*. Another popular classification scheme uses the terms *classified, secret*, and *top secret*. While the actual terms will vary from company to company, it is important that they distinguish categories clearly. You must also consider the effects of data aggregation. Individual elements of relatively low-level data, when combined, may actually be very sensitive.

Some companies will put a dollar amount on the risk of losing a piece of sensitive data. For example, if a customer record is hacked, the cost of disclosure is X dollars. While this can be a good way to procure a security budget, it can also be misused. A new pilot project with a limited number of records, even if insecure, would have minimal impact if, say, only 50 records were involved. A risk rating system based purely on the potential dollar loss impact would rate such a test project as being of minimal risk. The exact same project, rolled into full production with millions of customer records, would be of a much higher risk. This change in project status could have serious implications if the risk was not re-evaluated in between and mitigated accordingly.

An assessment model that is based solely on potential dollar loss can lead to invalid risk assessments of pilot programs. The effectiveness of the actual security controls must be assessed in addition to the potential dollar loss.

In addition to classifying data based on its sensitivity, data also needs to be labeled based on retention requirements. Depending on the nature of the information, data may have legally mandated retention periods. Failure to maintain data for the required retention period could expose a company to serious legal ramifications. Imagine the implications of not being able to produce the required information for a government audit, or a judge's subpoena? As I've said before, this is not a job for amateurs.

As important as comprehensive security policies are, it's the adoption of such requirements that actually protects the data. The exercise of moving from documenting how your company is going to protect your data to actually protecting it requires a comprehensive defense-in-depth strategy. A good place to begin is with a well-thought-out network design.

CHAPTER 2

NETWORK/DMZ DESIGN

Some people in the industry say that as security increases both network and system performance decrease. The reality is that this is not a zero sum game, and it is axiomatic that a secure network is also one that is well thought out and efficient. There is also a saying that goes, "Build it for dime or fix it for a dollar." Building a secure network is much less expensive than making a network secure. A recurring theme throughout this book will be to show how companies can maximize the return on their security investments (ROSI). It is also fair to say that a network that is continually infected with viruses or compromised by hackers isn't very efficient. In this chapter, we'll look at how to build efficiency and security into your network environments.

DEMILITARIZED ZONES

A Demilitarized Zone (DMZ) is a segment of a network that is separated from the rest of the network by a firewall. There are numerous different ways that a DMZ can be implemented. Some companies will use a single firewall to protect both their Internet-facing Web servers as well as their internal networks. A multi-homed or multi-interfaced firewall is a single physical device used to "protect" multiple network segments. This could include the same firewall being used for an Internet DMZ, as well as the internal part of a company's network. An old adage says, "It isn't a matter of if your Internet Web servers will be hacked, but when." Relying on a single firewall to protect your internal network from the Internet is asking for trouble.

A more traditional type of DMZ typology can be referred to as a sandwich design. It consists of an outer firewall that faces the Internet, and an inner firewall that separates the DMZ—the middle of the sandwich—from your internal network. DMZ environments should be considered semi-trusted because the systems in a DMZ are either accessed by the general public or by business partners and vendors from the Internet. As such, they are considered more vulnerable to attack than a company's internal network, which is protected by the internal firewall.

FIREWALL TECHNOLOGIES

A good way to add a level of security to your network without incurring a lot of extra expense is to deploy different types of firewalls. Have one type of firewall for your outward facing perimeter, which consists of the firewalls that face either the Internet or companies with which you have dedicated connections. Dedicated connections like these are also known as extranets. Have a different type for the internal firewalls, or those that separate your DMZ from your internal network. If you're going to use a traditional DMZ typology, you are going to have to purchase inner and outer firewalls anyway. By using two different types of firewalls, you now force the would-be hacker to do twice the work. The goal is not to try to become "hack proof," but rather, "hack resistant." The vast majority of hackers will look for the easy target. This is a cost-effective way to avoid making your network that easy target.

DEMILITARIZED ZONES BY FUNCTION

Depending on the size of your company's network, having dedicated DMZs based on their function is an approach to consider. There are many different ways to separate DMZs. You could create dedicated DMZs for e-mail, Web servers, extranets, virtual private networks, etc. Some companies separate their DMZs even further by operating system, having different areas for UNIX-based and Windows-based servers. The benefit is that a DMZ segmented in this manner would allow engineers who are specialized on one platform to concentrate on systems built on that platform and not have to dabble in another. Changes to the configuration of one type of server in a DMZ could inadvertently cause issues to servers that use a different operating system. Throughout my career, I have met very talented engineers skilled in UNIX, Windows, and mid-range systems such as AS400's and mainframes. But I have yet to meet an engineer that is highly skilled in all types of systems.

Another approach is to separate DMZs by the data type contained within. By separating DMZs by data type, you don't unnecessarily endanger sensitive data by placing it in the same DMZ that contains systems with only low-grade information. This is particularly true when dealing with multiple third parties. Depending on the nature of the data, as well as the business relationships with the respective third parties, you want to ensure that one third party company doesn't get access to another's data. This could possibly result in breach of contract and non-disclosure issues. There could also be a dollar savings by having a one DMZ for systems containing sensitive data and another for those that do not. By concentrating the resources for extra security controls on the DMZ that contained the sensitive data, you would be spending dollars to protect the area with the greater risk.

Sometimes, a company may want to create a DMZ not because of the nature of the data contained on the servers, but because third parties have access to the systems. Such a solution would limit the access the third party had to those systems located in the DMZ itself, affording a level of protection to the rest of your company's network.

SERVER CONFIGURATION

Servers that are in DMZs and exposed to the outside world should be built with tighter security controls. Standards that mandate these controls are sometime referred to as bastion host standards. Since they are more vulnerable to attack, they need to be built to more stringent standards than servers that reside on a company's internal network. They should not share authentication services (username and password) with trusted hosts within the network. This way, if a bastion host is compromised, the intruder will not have the "keys to the kingdom."

A bastion host is "hardened" to limit potential methods of attack. The specific steps to harden a particular bastion host depend upon the intended role of that server as well as the operating system and software that it will be running. They will vary depending on whether the system is running a version of Windows or UNIX, and whether it's an Internet-facing Web server, an e-mail server, etc. Each bastion host should fulfill a specific role. This means all unnecessary services, programs, and network ports that are not relevant to that role are either disabled or removed as appropriate. Servers accept information on ports, which are akin to open doors in an office building. Servers should only accept the type of communications specific to their functions. For example, if a server does not handle FTP files as a part of its defined function, turn off the ports that accept that communication. In other words, lock the doors that nobody should be coming through.

Once a server has been built to security specifications, it must be routinely updated to maintain its secure posture. All appropriate service packs, hot fixes, and patches should be installed. Keep a record (a log) of all security-related events for forensics purposes. In addition to enabling logging, steps need to be taken to protect the logs themselves. A common measure is to keep the log files on a separate server altogether. Any local user account and password databases should be encrypted. A particular type of encryption called hashing, which utilizes one-way (non-reversible) encryption, is best for passwords. Hashes are considered harder to crack than "regular" encryption since by design they are non-reversible. Considering how sensitive passwords are, the tougher the controls the better.

The term bastion host is not limited to servers within a DMZ, but also applies to external firewalls and perimeter routers. They are exposed to the outside world, and hence are more vulnerable to attack. The guidance to ensure secure configuration applies to these systems as well.

MULTI-TIERED ARCHITECTURES

Another effective way to secure any sensitive data that is accessible from the Internet is by not placing it directly on a Web server itself. Use the Web server strictly as the face to the world, and store the actual data on another system, such as a database server, on your company's internal network with a firewall placed between the two systems. If the Web server is compromised, the hacker will still have to break through the firewall and the back-end database server to access the data. This type of design is known as a two-tiered architecture. For an additional layer of security, you can place another system between the Web server and the database server. This is known as a three-tiered architecture. In this type of scenario, the third system is usually an application server that, among other things, can perform additional authentication control functions.

WHERE TO STORE SENSITIVE INFORMATION

One thing makes protecting sensitive data both more difficult and more expensive: It's the fact that to many companies have this information spread throughout their entire network on a wide range of systems. I've also seen just about every type of database software known to man deployed in a single network. Since most encryption solutions will not work on every type of system, this makes protecting the data more difficult, not to mention more expensive. Companies are forced to find multiple solutions to protect the sensitive data that they have residing on their Access, DB2, Oracle, SQL, and Teradata systems, to name but a few.

How much could you save if your company just had two or three database types to encrypt instead of, say, fifteen? Consider the dollar saving potential of a policy that required sensitive data to reside on a well-defined, finite set of server operating systems and database types. How much money could be saved if your company only had to worry about encrypting data on either the latest version of Oracle on UNIX or SQL on Windows? There could be other cost savings as well, including reduced maintenance and support fees as well as volume pricing discounts from suppliers. A company that restricts which sensitive data can reside on which types of systems is better able to ensure that those systems are configured and maintained to the highest security standards.

The more heterogeneous (varied) a network, the harder and more expensive it is to maintain. You'll be forced to hire more engineers to ensure a knowledge base that knows how to properly administer the different types of systems. Interoperability may be an issue, since some systems intrinsically don't communicate well with others. Limiting the types of servers and applications that are used within your company's network is therefore not only more secure, it is also more efficient and less expensive.

WHERE TO LOCATE SERVERS

Companies should limit where, on network servers, sensitive data can reside. This allows a company to put extra security controls in place to protect those systems. For instance, if individuals from a third party had access to your company's internal network, they could be blocked from the areas of the network that had servers with sensitive data. This is much more difficult and may even be impossible to do if sensitive data resides on every type of system throughout the entire network. You should also require all systems that contain sensitive data to be placed in hardened data centers.

Systems with non-sensitive data can exist efficiently in an administrative facility. For example, a server that contains marketing brochures could be housed in a secured room in the same building where your company's marketing personnel are located. This would likely increase network response times for your marketing personnel, while at the same time freeing up the more expensive floor space in your data center for systems that contained sensitive data. While a server room in an administrative facility is not as secure as a full-blown data center, don't forget the principle that you should devote more resources to the environment with the most risk. The risk is generally with the data itself, so focus your money and energies on protecting data that is either classified as sensitive or high value to your company.

SEGREGATION OF TEST AND DEVELOPMENT SERVERS

The test and development parts of any network should be separate from the production environment. Co-mingling test and development environments with production systems can have a negative impact on the confidentiality, integrity, and availability of data. The security measures in a test environment are not usually on par with those found in a production environment.

Stringent security controls can have a negative impact on the actual development process. By definition, test and development environments are in a constant state of flux, with engineers manipulating applications, making changes to data, and so on. The change-control processes that are used to protect production systems would hamper those testing and development activities. So you have frequent changes that are not subject to the same level of oversight as in a production environment. To make matters worse, any engineer that has spent time working in a test and development environment knows that "accidents" happen quite frequently. A change that does not function as anticipated can result in lost data or in a system crash. This isn't necessarily a bad thing and is actually part of the learning process involved in the test and development world. However, if co-mingled with a production environment, such activities can cause outages to production systems and interruptions to critical business functions, costing the company money and other resources.

Do not risk the loss of an entire database in the name of testing the latest feature. Even fully tested upgrades released by the manufacturer may still not be compatible with your company's servers. This is because the manufacturer is not testing its upgrades on systems identical to the ones that are running within your company's network. Your production support engineers don't want their systems to crash because a developer applied an untested piece of software on the server.

System outages, data loss, or even changes to data that lead to invalid outputs can be disruptive. It is common for companies to test security patches and updates to anti-virus files prior to applying them to production systems. If your test systems reside on the production network, this type of due diligence is not possible. It is a frequent practice to test numerous patches and fixes at any given time. Perform this type of work in a production environment and you could cause an outage that would be hard to troubleshoot. In this scenario, the outage could have been caused by any singe patch or by a combination of patches. Where do you begin troubleshooting? I have seen a single server used for both production and test and development. Its hard drives had one partition (section) for production, while another was for test and development. Any testing that might crash the server would also impact production. The odds of a developer inadvertently affecting production when the only separation is a partition on a hard drive are likely to be very good. As a rule, test and development networks should be separated from production networks.

TEST WITH TEST DATA

Data used in test and development should not be live production data, especially if it is sensitive information. Use dummy, or scrubbed, data instead. Dummy data is information that is fictitious to begin with. Scrubbed data is live data that has had sensitive aspects removed while maintaining the integrity required for testing purposes. There are numerous data scrubbing applications available on the market today. Companies such as Oracle Corporation, Ascential Software Corporation, Group 1 Software, SAS Institute, and Informatica Corporation all sell data-scrubbing software. Most major data warehouse and business-intelligence vendors also include data-scrubbing features in their products. The particular solution that is right for you will depend on the technical specifics of your company's network.

Bear in mind that an application needs only to test the characteristics of data, and not the true values. For instance, 123-45-6789 fits the parameters of a social security number without exposing any real, sensitive data. It is the data parameters that are important in most cases, and not the true information itself. Nonetheless, there are instances, such as in the case of statistical modeling, in which you need to use live data to generate valid outputs. When testing a new statistical modeling application, your test environment should have sufficient security controls to protect even a small amount of sensitive information.

A mature software development lifecycle entails, among other things, good version control. If you have numerous engineers working on developing the same application, you need a way to keep track of the most recent version. It is even good to lock an application, effectively blocking other developers from making changes, until the engineer currently making changes has completed his or her work. Concurrent Versions System, or CVS, is one of many software tools available that can help maintain version control when more than one engineer is developing an application.

VENDOR ACCESS

Companies are often required to grant representatives from vendor companies access to their internal networks for legitimate business purposes. The challenge in this situation is how to implement proper security measures. The first question to ask is, how much access is necessary to achieve the desired results? Many companies rely on third parties to provide support for their systems. Such support can be as simple as making a phone call to Microsoft for support with a Windows-based system or to another vendor that supports a proprietary application on one of your servers.

There are many different ways that a third party can provide technical support. Many vendors will say that they *require* remote access into systems in order to provide the requisite level of support, often with high levels of privileged access. Granting this type of access is very risky, and you should not permit it whenever possible. Remember, you are the customer. You should not allow a company that wants your business to dictate these types of terms. Support methods that are far less risky include both phone support and escorted, on-site visits to work on a system. Technical manuals, both physical and online, are also great resources. You should also require third parties to provide training for the proprietary systems that they are trying to sell you.

If you must give a vendor remote access to a system for support purposes, there are protective measures that reduce your risk. First of all, I strongly recommend not allowing connections via modem. Most modems transmit data in clear text, and are easily hacked. If your company has a virtual private network (VPN), require that your third parties use that whenever possible. Insist that they only be given the level of access necessary to perform their support functions. Many will insist that they need highly privileged accounts. In most instances, such access is usually not required and is generally just laziness on the part of the third party. High-level access meets their needs and does not require them to put any thought or effort into determining the precise level of access that is actually required. Least privileged access is a cornerstone to effective data security. Modern operating systems are capable of granting access on very specific levels. Only give vendors the access that they truly require. If they can't tell you the precise level of access that they need, you may want to ask yourself how well they understand the product that they are trying to sell you.

I was once told by a third party supporting a piece of database software that they would need to be sent the entire contents of the database, data and all, in order to troubleshoot any problems. I refused. But it's an excellent example of what I call "lazy engineering." Give me anything I could possibly need to get my job done, says the lazy engineer, rather than requiring me to determine what is actually necessary. You can restrict a vendor's remote access to your systems in other ways as well. If your company has its own VPN solution, require vendors to use it for their remote access, as opposed to modems or their own VPN solution.

Require vendors to use a secure ID/fob as part of your company's VPN solution (this is discussed more in Chapter 4). Use secure ID/fobs that have serial numbers on them. This way, your company can maintain a record of which vendor personnel have been issued which ID/fob. For an added level of security, vendor's ID/fobs can be disabled. If they only need access to provide production support on an as-needed basis, restrict their access to only those instances. It would only take a phone call from an authorized employee to have your company's VPN support group activate the ID/fob when needed.

Consider leaving the vendor's user account, on the server that they provide support for, disabled as well. Enable it only when the vendor's people need access to provide technical support. You may also consider issuing the vendor a one-time username/password combination. This is also known as a firecall ID. When they activate their remote access, they are given this one-time firecall ID. The security benefit is simple: once they've completed their work, they can't reuse the single-use ID.

WIRELESS

Something that most end-users love, and makes most security professionals cringe, is having a wireless network within a company's network environment. Integrating a wireless component into your company's wired network can introduce a whole host of security issues. Wireless offers the lure of easy access without the expense and hassle of having to install network cabling. Unfortunately, the same ease of connectivity it gives to your employees is also afforded to hackers, unless appropriate security controls are put in place.

There are many security measures that should be included when deploying wireless. An obvious one is encryption. I recommend using the strongest wireless encryption available, which as of this writing is Wi-Fi Protected Access-2 (WPA-2). I also recommend using filtering on your wireless access points, which allows only the computers that are registered on the system to gain access. This can be done with a computer's IP address or even its MAC address. A MAC address, the address of a computer's network card, is better to use since most end-user systems don't have static IP addresses. Rather, they commonly use a technology called Dynamic Host Configuration Protocol, or DHCP. It's a system that assigns an IP address from an identified range for a specific "lease" period. At the end of the lease period, a different IP address within the range is assigned. Thus, if you filter by IP address, you would have to update the filter every time the addresses change. Filtering by MAC address is also more secure because it is possible for hackers to try and trick IP filters. They will assign an IP address for their rogue systems to match that of one on the approved list. This is known as IP spoofing.

The physical placement of the wireless access point is also important. Access points should be placed in a manner that limits the wireless network's range to include only your company's facility. This can be problematic, especially if you share a building with other companies. Since, by their nature, wireless access points have to be placed near workers and not in a hardened server room, physical security becomes an issue as well.

A hacker could place a rogue wireless access point either in or near your company's building and gain access to your entire network. Hiding a wireless access point in a drop ceiling, a utility closet, or even behind bushes adjacent to the building could therefore let a hacker gain access to your company's network. This situation could also cause your employees to connect to the hacker's rogue wireless access point instead of your company's network. The hacker only needs to trick your employees long enough to have them log on. The hacker would then have a real username and password to enable him to log on to servers on your company's network. Wireless should be considered only semi-trusted at best, and as such placed in a DMZ that requires users to pass through a firewall prior to gaining access to a company's internal systems.

As you can see, the controls required to offer even minimal security for wireless begin to strip away any cost savings. Perhaps one of the most serious security implications of allowing wireless into a company's network is that it would mean having wireless access capabilities on your employees' workstations and laptops. While the convenience of being able to work from the local coffee shop may be very metropolitan, it is also very insecure. In such a scenario, employees are using the coffee shop's wireless network. A wireless network designed for use by the public by nature can't use either filtering or encryption, since both would block access to some users. If a VPN is required for access to your company's network, that would provide protection for data in transit. However, the data on the laptop itself would still be at risk. Even simple Web browsing from an unsecured wireless network will put the data on your laptop at risk. A lot of employees browse the Internet without using the VPN, thereby effectively bypassing any Web site filtering your company may have. So in addition to the risk of hacking, there's also the risk of going to unapproved Web sites.

It is possible to configure a laptop's VPN software so that it is initiated automatically upon detecting any connectivity to the Internet. If company laptops have wireless capability, I highly recommend using this type of solution.

WEB BROWSING

I encourage companies to place controls on where their employees can go on the Internet, and to both monitor and log such activity. Certain types of Internet traffic are bandwidth intensive, such as streaming video, and can have a negative impact on a network's performance. There is also the issue of inappropriate Web sites, or even employees spending an inordinate amount of time surfing the Web instead of doing their job. There are solutions available that can monitor what sites employees are accessing on the Internet, and even block access to predetermined sites. Companies such as Websense have software that can be loaded directly on an end user's system, so the policies will be enforced whether they're attached to your company's network or not.

No single security measure is the magic bullet to protecting your company's sensitive data. Truly effective data security requires a defense-in-depth approach to provide multiple layers of protection and the maximum level of safety. This is even more important in those instances when the data is highly sensitive or when a particular security measure cannot be utilized due to a technical limitation.

CHAPTER 3

DEFENSE IN DEPTH

Defense in depth, also known as a layered defense, is the best way to protect your company's network and the data it contains. There are numerous perils in relying on a single technology to protect your entire network. To illustrate this point, ask yourself if your network's protective posture is like a burnt marshmallow or a burnt piece of toast. A burnt marshmallow is hard on the outside but has a soft chewy center, while burnt toast is hard all the way through. In network-security terms, the analogy illustrates the peril of relying too heavily on perimeter security controls (such as firewalls). Doing so turns your network into a burnt marshmallow, making it vulnerable if a hacker gets inside.

The hard reality is that no single security measure is the end-all to protecting your company's data. Humanity has yet to invent either a technical or a physical deterrent that is impossible to overcome. That is why there is no such thing as the absence of risk. The ideal approach needs to be a well-thought-out combination of complementary security measures. Ideally, a defense-in-depth posture will thwart most hackers and sufficiently slow down the truly determined ones so they are detected before they can do any harm. There is value in limiting the potential damage that a highly skilled hacker can cause, and there are dividends in being able to show that your company is a responsible steward for its sensitive data. When considering where to spend your data security dollars, it is important to define what you are trying to accomplish. Different security measures can deal with suspicious activity in a multitude of ways.

DETECTIVE, REACTIVE, AND PREVENTATIVE CONTROLS

All security measures have their strengths and their weaknesses. The security industry tends to group controls in one of three categories. Some are detective and only serve to provide a warning that a bad event has happened. Others are reactive and perform a corrective action after the

Table 3.1: Security Controls *Adapted from Government of Hong Kong information*

Type of Control	Preventive	Detective	Reactive
Administrative			
security awareness training	X	X	
monitoring & supervising	X	X	X
personnel procedures	X	X	X
clearly identified roles and responsibilities	X		X
comprehensive security policy	X		X
Physical			
regular backups (test restores)		X	X
badge system (photo – contact – proximity)	X		X
security cameras (CCTV)	X	X	X
Technical			
automated alarms/alerts		X	
anti-virus software	X	X	X
audit & event logs		X	
encryption	X		X
firewalls	X	X	X
spam filtering software	X	X	X

event has occurred. Those that fall into the third category are labeled as preventative and try to stop the event from occurring. A single device can fall into multiple categories, depending on its configuration. Table 3.1 contains a list of some of the three different types of controls, further categorized by whether they are administrative, technical, or physical in nature.

Passive systems are those that strictly detect potentially illegitimate activity without taking an action beyond generating an alert. Active devices are those that, upon detecting illegitimate traffic, take some sort of action to stop it.

FIREWALLS

Utilizing a layered defense is what affords a company the most comprehensive security. Most people, even those without much exposure to the data security field, have heard of firewalls. Properly deployed and configured, firewalls can be a very strong defensive resource. However, they do have their weaknesses. Some firewall technologies do not handle certain types of network traffic very well. Multicast traffic, a type of transport communication protocol that sends data from one system out to many others (referred to as "one-to-many"), can cause problems for the stateful-inspection type of firewall. Any firewall, no matter the technology, is only as good as the firewall rules programmed into it, which dictate what network traffic gets through. If the rules are too broad or not configured properly, it can create a very large security hole directly into your company's network.

Firewall rules should be as specific as possible, limiting both the number of IP addresses as well as the number of open ports that allow the appropriate traffic to pass through them. Computer systems have IP addresses, while data is transmitted over ports. A good analogy would be to think of an IP address as your home's physical location and the ports as the different windows and doors granting entry. A home with a hundred open doors and windows is more likely to be burglarized.

Some transport protocols by design require a large number of open ports in order to be able to traverse a firewall successfully. Remote Procedure Call, RPC, is a good example of this point. A commonly held belief is that RPC needs all high ports, those above 1,023, in order to properly operate through a firewall. However, it is possible to limit the number of ports that have to be opened to allow RPC to traverse a firewall. This can be accomplished by determining the maximum number of possible concurrent connections that will be used, and multiplying that number by two. So, if the maximum number of concurrent connections is 100, you only need to open 200 ports, or perhaps a few more, say 230, to allow for some slack space. That is certainly better than opening 64,511 ports, the total number above 1,023. With a little additional effort, you can force RPC through that more narrowly defined range of ports. This extra work can result in a significant reduction of risk. Another way to eliminate the risks associated with RPC is to have a policy stating that this particular protocol is not allowed to traverse your company's firewalls. If the system the firewall is installed on isn't properly configured, it may be hacked, which in turn would compromise the firewall itself.

As mentioned in the last chapter, deploying different types of firewall technologies adds a layer of defense in and of itself. Having your outward-facing firewalls be a different type of technology than your inner ones means that the would-be hacker has to compromise two types of firewalls in order to gain access to your company's inner network. I would recommend using a combination of two of the following types of firewall technologies: a proxy-based firewall, an application firewall, and a stateful-inspection firewall. These types of firewalls all have their different strengths that, when used in tandem, make for an effective security control.

ROUTERS

Perimeter routers with properly configured access control lists, ACLs, are another defensive measure. Router ACLs determine what traffic a router will allow to pass. Since perimeter routers are also positioned at the outer edge of a network, they need to be protected as well. While routers can be an effective security control, a router is not a firewall and shouldn't be used as such. Do not try to save money by relying on your company's perimeter routers as your sole security measure. That doesn't even qualify as a burnt marshmallow. It would be more like lightly browned.

AUDIT FIREWALLS AND ROUTERS

Performing regular audits of both firewall rules and router access control lists is critical. Any rules that are no long needed should be deleted. This takes a certain level of understanding of your company's network traffic. Most firewall rules that haven't been used for more than 90 days would be good candidates for deletion. Proper procedures need to be in place to ensure that required rules aren't accidentally deleted, which could block business critical network traffic. Maintain a log of the deleted records for a specified period so they can be put back if necessary. In addition to keeping a log of the successful use of firewall rules, you should also keep track of traffic that your firewalls block. This may be an indication that a hacker is attempting to gain access into your network.

SECURITY AND APPLICATIONS

Many vendors will try to sell insecure applications to companies that house sensitive data. And they sometimes try to force companies to make security concessions to allow their applications to function within that company's environment. For example, some vendors will hard-code a system's IP address into the application. Most firewalls use a technology called network address translation, or NAT. For network traffic coming into your network, an Internet routable or outward facing IP address will be targeted. These outward-facing IP addresses are publicly registered, and can easily be identified as belonging to your company. NAT is the process of taking that traffic, and changing the outward facing IP to the non-Internet routable IP address of the target system on your company's internal network. (For the engineers reading this, Internet routable IP addresses follow RFC 1918.)

The vendor will insist that its application be allowed to traverse your company's firewalls without being NATted. I recommend a different approach. If a vendor wants to do business with a company that houses sensitive data, they should make sure that their products or service models are built with security in mind. There's a saying in security that goes, "In God we trust; everybody else we verify." No vendor will ever tell you that their products are not secure, or that the application they are trying to sell you is riddled with exploits that will put your network at risk. They are not being openly dishonest; it's just that many companies lack the specific expertise to know if their products are secure or not. Certainly, most sales representatives are not security experts.

PROBLEMATIC PROTOCOLS

I do not want to leave the topic of firewalls and protocols without mentioning some other issues beyond RPC. There are other protocols that, by their very nature, should not be allowed to traverse your company's perimeter firewalls. Protocols that can be used by a hacker to map the interior part of a network, such as PING and Traceroute, which are both part of a family of Internet Control Message Protocols (ICMP), should be blocked. While PING and Traceroute are both very effective for troubleshooting network connectivity issues, they can also be used by a hacker to try to gather data. There are entire books devoted to the security implications of ICMP-based protocols. I will sum it up by saying that policies that control the use of such protocols need to be developed by consulting with engineers who are experts in this area. It is also a cornerstone of good security to provide only the required information. If a third party wants to be able to use PING to test connectivity with your network, let them PING only to the outside of your firewall. That will test connectivity from their network to the outside of your network. There are other tools that you can use to test connectivity from that point without letting a third party's PING traffic fully traverse your firewalls.

Protocols such as Network File System (NFS), which could allow a hacker to connect to, or mount, a shared drive on a server, should not be allowed either. While there are many others, I mention this to make the point that you want an engineer who is a security professional managing your company's firewalls, and not simply an administrator whose knowledge is limited to how to keep the system up and running.

FIREWALL AND ROUTER ADMINISTRATION

Passwords for both your firewalls and your routers should be changed frequently, probably at least every 60 days. Firewalls should also be configured with session timeouts. If an open connection has no traffic for a certain amount of time, it should be closed. This is particularly true if using stateful-inspection firewalls, whose main security control is whether or not a particular transmission was both opened and closed properly. Change any default accounts that came shipped with the firewall or router before the device is placed into production. Engineers who work on such critical systems should either perform their work at the device itself or through an encrypted transport protocol, if accessing the systems remotely.

If remote access to critical systems such as perimeter firewalls is required, keep the list of approved users to a minimum. Audit the list of authorized users frequently, making any necessary changes. You may even want to consider requiring two-factor authentication (discussed in Chapter 4) to access such sensitive systems. I would strongly discourage any company from outsourcing the administration of their firewalls or routers to a third-party service provider. You would be, in essence, turning over the keys to your entire network to them. Aside from the security implications, if an edge router or a perimeter firewall were to go down, it could break the ability of your company's computer network to communicate with the outside world. If you sell your products online, this could have a huge impact. Your company would be at the mercy of the third-party service provider to resolve the issue, during which time you would be literally closed for business.

INTRUSION DETECTION SENSORS (IDS)

Network-based intrusion detection is yet another tool to provide added depth to your company's perimeter defenses. Intrusion detection sensors, or IDS, can be either signature-based or anomaly-based. Signature-based IDS works off of known bad items. Network traffic that security engineers have defined as inappropriate gets documented and logged. Those known definitions of inappropriate network traffic are referred to as signatures. As new bad signatures are discovered by their administrators, they should be added to the IDS sensor to keep it current. On the other hand, anomaly-based IDS sensors work by identifying "unusual" behavior. To know what is considered "unusual," these types of IDS sensors must be programmed to recognize normal network activity.

There is more of a learning process with anomaly-based IDS sensors. If you make them overly sensitive, they will generate alerts for legitimate traffic. This is also known as a Type I error, or a false positive. On the other hand, an anomaly-based IDS sensor that isn't sensitive enough will allow bad traffic to pass without generating any kind of alarm. This is known as a Type II error, or a false negative. A properly calibrated anomaly-based

IDS sensor will have a crossover rate, which indicates the level to which both types of error rates are minimized. Depending on the environment and your company's sensitivity to detecting illegitimate traffic, a higher frequency of one type of error or another may be desirable.

There are also intrusion prevention sensors that go beyond detecting suspicious traffic to actually blocking it in real time. Intrusion prevention sensors (IPS) were invented in the late 1990s. The industry sees them as a considerable improvement upon firewall technologies, as they can make access control decisions based on application content rather than IP address or ports, as traditional firewalls do.

ENCRYPTION

Encryption is an important part of any defense-in-depth strategy. This importance can be ascribed to the fact that many governmental regulations mandating the protection of data rely heavily on encryption. This has lead to companies relying on encryption, as well as a rush by vendors to create more encryption solutions. As mentioned, a way to reduce the cost of encrypting data is to store sensitive information only on a limited number of well-defined types of systems. This makes finding encryption solutions much easier. There are some encryption solutions that are operating system agnostic. In other words, they consist of separate hardware devices that don't care what type of system the data is stored on. Decru and Neoscale are two examples of separate hardware encryption devices. This can also help with system performance as the work of encrypting the data, which is CPU intensive, occurs on a separate device rather than on the server itself. Some of these devices are locked and will delete their encryption keys if they are forced open. This feature may actually be required, depending on the industry you're in and the nature of the data you are trying to protect. While this is a good way to logically protect encryption keys, it makes the physical protection of those devices very important.

Newer versions of most database solutions provide field-level encryption. This would allow a company to encrypt only those fields that contain sensitive data. Implementing encryption in this method is much more efficient then encrypting the entire contents of a database. Encrypting the entire contents of a database could potentially have serious performance implications and may even cause systems to fail. When encrypting sensitive data that is stored on your company's computers, don't forget the data that you send off-site on backup tapes. If the data is important enough to encrypt while at your company, it should be encrypted while on backup tape as well. This is particularly true when you consider the capacity of backup tapes. Bear in mind that just one tape can contain millions of sensitive records. Even if the data on your backup tapes are encrypted, you should maintain a strong chain of custody and use only locked containers when transporting them. I also recommend that you perform routine audits of your off-site tape storage facility to ensure all of your company's backup tapes are accounted for. The wrong time to learn that a tape is missing is when you need that backup tape to restore data that has been lost.

WHEN ENCRYPTION IS INSECURE

All of the technologies mentioned above can be foiled. And not just by an ingenious hacker, but also by implementing certain types of connectivity that may seem secure at first, but which can actually add risk. For example, allowing a third party to have an encrypted transmission from their network all the way through to your internal network can be dangerous. You may think that this would add to the security of your network, but it can actually create a large problem. Intrusion detection sensors cannot inspect encrypted traffic. The same technology that protects the confidentiality of the data foils the IDS system. An even worse situation would be to allow a company to use a transport protocol like SSH (Secure Shell) from their network right into your internal network. In addition to being an encrypted transport protocol, SSH is also interactive and allows other protocols to tunnel through it. In essence, with SSH, a hacker could send any information past the intrusion detection sensors. They would be able to tunnel *any* traffic right through a company's firewalls. Since SSH is interactive, the hacker could try to actively control (interact with) a system remotely.

While conventional wisdom states that encryption always protects data, it is a tool like anything else: if improperly utilized, it can actually make a network less secure. Some third parties will want to use their VPN solution to access your company's computers. As with SSH, this would have the same effect of bypassing intrusion detection sensors—not being able to inspect what data a vendor may be taking from (or inserting on) your systems. If a vendor refuses to use your company's VPN solution, or insists on using modems or other things that would put your company's data at risk, perhaps they are not the best vendor with which to do business. This is particularly true for companies that have data that is heavily regulated, such as the health care and financial services industries. Sensitive areas of the government would not permit this type of access by vendors. Here in the United States, in most cases, if there is one company providing a particular product or service, dozens of other companies are likely doing the same thing. Do not let companies that are trying to do business with you dictate terms that put your company at risk. In some cases, the vendor is a hard-to-move 800-pound gorilla. In these cases, I have seen competitors in the same industry band together to increase their bargaining power when trying to get security concessions from the larger vendor.

SERVER CONFIGURATION

Secure server configurations and regular patch management are integral to a strong defense-in-depth posture. The Trusted Computer System Evaluation Criteria, TCSEC, has a rating system, also known as the Orange Book, that ranks different levels of secure configurations for system builds. The more secure your system configurations are, the harder they are to hack. More importantly, however, is the fact that the stronger your system configurations are, the harder it will be for the would-be hacker to use them as launching points to gain access to other systems on your network. For example, if a given server is not using File Transport Protocol (FTP) as part of its normal functions, turn off the ports on the servers that listen for FTP. You may even want to disable or delete the FTP service on the system.

FILE TRANSPORT PROTOCOL (FTP)

While FTP is an efficient way to send and receive information, it transmits data unencrypted. There is also anonymous FTP, which allows users to access a machine without having to have a user account on it. So a Web server with anonymous FTP would, in essence, be accessible to anybody that had Internet access. This is not a very good way to protect your company's data. If sensitive data is going to be transmitted with FTP, I recommend encrypting the transmission using some other kind of technology. For example, Router-Based Encryption (RBE) will encrypt data while in transit from router to router. Some applications are available that will also encrypt the data, which is even better. Encryption applied at the application layer protects the data from the sending server to the receiving server and not just from router to router.

There are a couple of ways to implement FTP in a more secure fashion. FTPS, also known as FTPS/SSL, is an implementation of the standard FTP client with the added option of Secure-Socket Layer, SSL. SSL is the most common method used to transmit data over the Internet using encryption. Web sites whose URLs begin with HTTPS are generally using a form of SSL. There is also Secure FTP, or SFTP, which is a program that uses Secure Shell (SSH) to transfer files. Another option available to securely transmit FTP files is by using an application called WS-FTP Professional. WS-FTP Professional uses 256-bit AES to encrypt data in transit over both SSL and SSH. It also provides for file integrity by using SHA512, which is a one-way (non-reversible) encryption algorithm, also known as a hash.

BUDGET FOR SECURITY

One of the biggest mistakes a company can make is not factoring in security costs when funding its overall technology expenditures. In many instances, companies with centralized technology groups give those technology groups the ability to charge the business units they support for security-related functions, such as needing the services of a firewall engineer, or placing a server into a DMZ. Such centralized technology groups within a given organization are often a monopoly, and charge fees that far exceed the market rate for similar services. This often forces the business units to obtain extra funding for the security needs of their respective projects, or have them choose between functionality and security. At a minimum, it causes ill feelings on behalf of the business units toward the technology group, because now their project is either in jeopardy or over-budget.

Wherever possible, have all security- and technology-related services be paid for out of base budgeting. Forcing projects to have to decide whether or not they have the budget to be secure is a poor security model. You also do not want to miss out on a new business opportunity because there wasn't enough money to pay for all the expenses of the technology groups. Internally, at a high level, it's all a shell game. At the company level, you're only moving funds from one group's budget to another. On the other hand, missing out on a business opportunity or compromising security can have a real impact enterprise-wide.

COMPUTER FORENSICS

When something bad happens, like a data breach or some other kind of illegal or inappropriate activity, it's important to be able to legally document the event. Computer forensics, an evidence-gathering exercise similar to a criminal investigation that a police officer or a crime lab would perform, is a specialized field of study. Proper forensic procedures are important, because if a computer system is deemed to be altered in any way, any information on the system could lose its evidentiary value in a court of law. In addition to the data in question needing to be a true and exact representation of what is on the original system, there must also be a strong chain of custody. Just as a police officer will place physical evidence of a crime under lock and key, any evidence in a computer case must be protected as well. Proper computer forensics can even determine if a suspected breach actually did occur or what data, if any, was actually stolen. Depending on the nature of the data, and the prevailing laws, this knowledge can save your company millions of dollars in fines and penalties, and limit the scope of any disclosure requirements.

There are certifications in the field of computer forensics. These are people who are not only qualified to conduct such an investigation, but can also testify in a court of law as an expert witness. It is also very important to be cognizant of the specific legal requirements of the jurisdiction in which your company resides in order to ascertain which certifications qualify certified individuals to be legally recognized computer forensics experts. With that said, the following are some certifications:

C3C—Certified Cyber-Crime Expert

The C3C identifies computer forensics investigators in professions such as law enforcement, law, and corporate IT security as having the requisite skills necessary to obtain, manage, and preserve evidence of a computer (cyber) crime. This is important when testifying in a court of law, and having the evidence that has been collected to be considered admissible in court as well. Requirements include passing a course and two exams.

CCCI—Certified Computer Crime Investigator (Basic and Advanced)

The CCCI is another forensics certification that is used by both law enforcement and corporate IT security professionals. The requirements for the Basic CCCI certification include two years of experience. A college degree may be substituted for one of the years of experience. Additional requirements include a year and a half of investigations experience, plus 40 hours of computer crimes training as well as having no less than 10 investigations under one's belt.

CCE—Certified Computer Examiner

The CCE is a computer forensics certification that is offered by the Southeast Cybercrime Institute at Kennesaw State University. The University partnered with Key Computer Service in the development of the requirements of the CCE. The certification identifies people as having expertise in the field of computer forensics to include activities such as evidence gathering, handling, and storage. To obtain the CCE, candidates must pass an online test, as well as a hands-on, practical exercise.

CCFT—Certified Computer Forensic Technician (Basic and Advanced)

Similar to the Certified Computer Crime Investigator, the CCFT has both a basic as well as an advanced level. It is primarily targeted at law enforcement and IT security professionals specializing in computer forensics. The basic certification includes having a minimum of three years of experience. A college degree and one year of experience is also acceptable. Furthermore, to obtain a basic CCFT, applicants must have at least 18 months of forensics experience as well as 40 hours of computer forensics training, and must have participated in a minimum of 10 cases. To obtain the advanced certification, you need three years of experience. Unlike with the basic requirement, a college degree will only substitute for one of those years of experience. Additional requirements for the advanced designation include: four years of investigations, 80 hours of training, and involvement in 60 cases, 20 of which must have been in the role of the lead investigator.

CCISM—Certified Counterespionage and Information Security Manager

The CCISM is designed to prepare individuals to be able to identify potential sources of threats, and to defeat such attacks. Considered a management-level certification, the CCISM is also targeted to the executive who is managing an information security program at an organizational level.

CCSA—Certification in Control Self-Assessment

Regulations such Sarbanes-Oxley mandate that companies (publicly traded ones with SOX), conduct internal self-assessments to ensure the accuracy of their financial reporting. SOX also mandates that companies demonstrate that they have controls in place to protect the integrity and confidentiality of the systems used in making the financial reporting. The CCSA is for individuals who conduct such self-assessments.

CEECS—Certified Electronic Evidence Collection Specialist Certification

Unlike a number of the other certifications, the CEECS certification does not have any prerequisites with regard to either formal university education, companion security/technology certifications, or real-world experience. To obtain a CEECS, a candidate must successfully complete the CEECS certification course, which covers evidence gathering, as well as technical terminology, theory, and techniques.

CERI-ACFE—Advanced Computer Forensic Examination

Designed for law enforcement personnel, the CERI-ACFE certification identifies those peace officers who have advanced computer crime investigations experience and training. The basic requirement includes having two years of computer investigations and debugging experience on a Microsoft platform, as well as two years on a non-Microsoft platform. Beyond the real world experience, to obtain the CERI-ACFE certification, candidates must take 80 hours of approved training and successfully pass a written examination and a hands-on practical exercise.

CERI-ACSS—Advanced Computer System Security

Also designed for law enforcement personnel, the CERI-ACSS is for peace officers with advanced computer crime investigation training and experience. Requirements for the CERI-ACSS include having a minimum of two years of computer investigation and debugging experience, three years of working with the Microsoft platform, as well as one year on non-Microsoft platforms. Additional requirements include 40 hours of approved training, successfully passing both a written examination as well as a hands-on practical exercise.

CERI-CFE—Computer Forensic Examination

The CERI-CFE is the basic certification partner to the more advanced CERI-ACSS certification, both of which are offered by Cyber Enforcement Resources, Inc. The requirements for the CERI-CFE include having a minimum of two years of computer investigation and debugging, one year of working on the Microsoft platform, along with six months on a non-Microsoft platform. Additional requirements include 40 hours of approved trainingand successfully passing both a written examination and hands-on exercises.

CFCE—Certified Forensic Computer Examiner

Offered by the International Association of Computer Investigative Specialists (IACIS), the CFCE is a certification designed for both law enforcement and private IT security professionals alike. Requirements for the CFCE include passing both a written examination as well as a hands-on exercise as well.

CFE—Certified Fraud Examiner

The CFE is specifically targeted at both law enforcement and IT security professionals whose job is to detect financial fraud and other white-collar crimes. This certification would be of interest to industries such as financial institutions, securities trading, as well as other fields that have a legal mandate to perform audits to detect possible fraudulent or otherwise illegal financial transactions.

CHFI—Computer Hacking Forensic Investigator

The CHFI is targeted at professionals working in law enforcement, the Department of Defense, as well as information security professionals. Sponsored by the EC-Council, requirements include taking a class and passing a test.

CIA—Certified Internal Auditor

Not be confused with the Central Intelligence Agency, CIA in this context stands for Certified Internal Auditor. The Certified Internal Auditor is for professionals in the auditing field. However, the CIA is primarily targeted for individuals interested in auditing IT practices and procedures in additional to more traditional financial accounting.

CIFI—Certified Information Forensics Investigator

As with many of the other computer forensics certifications, the CIFI requires a minimum level of real world computer experience, as well as passing a test. As is common with many other of the certifications, adherence to a code of conduct and a clean record are required.

CSFA—CyberSecurity Forensic Analyst

The CSFA certification focuses on technology security issues, primarily at the hardware level. The prerequisites for the CSFA include having at least one existing computer certification. The certification can be in areas such as software support, networking, or security. The CSFA also require successful completion of both an introductory as well as an advanced-level computer forensics course that is offered through the CyberSecurity Institute. The CyberSecurity Institute is the issuing body for the CSFA.

Many of the certifications listed above require that applicants must have no criminal record. Practically speaking, the jobs that professionals holding these certifications usually have are positions of trust. As a result, it's still a good idea to do a background check.

VICARIOUS LIABILITY

Some companies do not have what they consider "sensitive" data. Many colleges and universities believe that security controls should be minimal in the name of academic freedom. If nothing else, employee and student records should be protected. Minimal security controls can also lead to the issue of vicarious liability. If a company is hacked, and they can show that the hacker used your unsecured systems to attack them, you can be held liable. Many hackers will use unsecured systems as zombies (computers that hackers have compromised) to launch their attacks for them. Using other systems as zombies not only increases attack power, it makes it harder for the authorities to trace the illegal act back to the actual hacker. While I am undoubtedly biased by being in the security field, I do believe that we need to try to ensure that our computer systems are secure enough, if for no other reason than to prevent them from being used to further the illegal activities of hackers or terrorists. Academic freedom and system security are not opposing forces.

USER-FRIENDLY SECURITY

It is one thing to require your employees to jump through security hoops to access sensitive data, but what about your external customers? For example, financial institutions that conduct business online aren't about to try to send out hardware tokens to their millions of customers to force them to use two-factor authentication to access their account online. There are ways to offer customers a reasonable level of security without causing them undue hassle. Requiring customers to enter a username and password is common. Some companies require their customers to use fairly complex passwords. This can trouble some customers and lead to a lot of account lockouts, necessitating a way for them to regain their access.

Some companies have their customers provide what is known as out-of-wallet information about themselves, which can be used to unlock their accounts. Examples of out-of-wallet information include: what city were you born in, what was the color of your first car, and what is your grandmother's maiden name? Another security measure is to allow your customers to receive their password in a predetermined e-mail account. This would require them to provide the e-mail account the first time they start using online services.

A security measure that is both effective and of no impact to the customer, is for the online system to capture system information, generally the IP address of the computer. If customers try to access an online account from a different computer, they could be required to answer some out-of-wallet questions to verify their identity. Consider having session timeouts after a predetermined period of inactivity. This would protect customers who forget to log out and leave their computers. This is particularly helpful for customers who choose to access the account from public computers. All of the controls that I have just mentioned would not be considered overly burdensome by most people, and yet provide a level of security to customers who are accessing their personal account information over the Internet. With the general level of awareness of credit card fraud and identity theft, most consumers would actually appreciate these types of security measures being taken on their behalf.

Consider the type of information that you are asking your customers to provide to gain access to their accounts online. Some companies use a customer's Social Security number as their username. Consider assigning your customers an account identifier, or allowing them to provide their own username. It provides the same level of security for the account number, without using a sensitive piece of data like a Social Security number.

E-MAIL SECURITY

There are numerous solutions on the market today to protect sensitive data while it is being e-mailed around the world. Three widely used solutions for their effectiveness and compatibility with most e-mail software clients include: Pretty Good Privacy (PGP), Public Key Infrastructure (PKI), and S/MIME. All of these solutions can encrypt data sent via e-mail to help ensure confidentiality. They also have functions to protect data integrity by being able to determine if the data has been altered. Functionality of these solutions can also include the ability to identify the sender to provide both authentication and non-repudiation. (Non repudiation is when a user can't deny that he or she actually sent the e-mail.) A weakness in PGP is that it uses what is known as a "web of trust." There is no single issuing authority verifying that the PGP encryption key is valid. A user could be using a key that had been hacked and may not know it. A hacker could use a stolen PGP encryption key to impersonate the legitimate owner. This is opposed to PKI, which has a single Certificate Authority that can issue and revoke keys.

A weakness of all three solutions is that it is up to the user to enable the encryption. The normal implementation is for e-mails to be sent in clear text unless the sender specifically takes action to encrypt the data. We humans are the weak link in the security chain, and in a large company, the chances for sensitive data to be e-mailed out in the clear are almost certain. There are solutions on the market today that send e-mail encrypted by default. They actually require the sender to take conscious action to send data out in clear text. I feel this model provides a better level of protection for the data, and is also more user-friendly. A sender forgetting to take the necessary action to not encrypt an e-mail is less of a risk than the reverse.

PHYSICAL SECURITY CONTROLS

In addition to technical controls for the data, you also need to consider physical controls for your company's facilities themselves. Data centers by definition generally house a large number of computer systems, ranging from mainframes to mid-ranges systems, as well as more widely used servers such as UNIX and Windows-based systems. Depending on their size, a data center can house hundreds or even thousands of computer systems, containing vast amounts of data. It is not unusual for companies to house nearly all of their sensitive information in data centers. So the actual physical protection of those facilities is paramount to the protection of your company's data.

The entrance to a data center should be tightly controlled. At an absolute minimum, access to a data center should be electronically logged. This means some kind of electronic access badge or a biometric system that could be tied back to each individual accessing the data center. Key access to highly sensitive areas should be limited to emergencies only, and should trigger an exception on a monitoring system in addition to being logged. Your company should tightly control the issuance of such keys. Remember, keys can be copied. Don't let your security rest on imprinting the words "do no copy" on the back of a brass key. Certain high security areas may even opt to use a sally port design. A sally port design consists of two sets of doors. The outer door has one type of access, and once you are past that you're in a small corridor that faces the inner door. Within that corridor there is a second access requirement to open the inner door into the actual data center itself. Only one set of doors can be opened at any give time. This prevents somebody from holding the outer doors open and then trying to open the inner doors, creating a clear path to the data center. Sally port corridors are sometimes weight sensitive, only permitting one person to pass through at a time.

You may also want to consider a system that prevent double backs. This means that once you go in a door, you must use your access to go out the door before you can go in the door again. This helps prevent people from holding the doors open for co-workers, which is known as tailgating. Courtesy is fine, but all employees should badge in where required to do so. In the event of an emergency like a fire, such a system would also help a company track their employees' whereabouts for evacuation purposes.

Any visitors being granted access to a data center should be escorted at all times. Their activities should be monitored, and items that they take in, as well as those they remove, should be subject to inspection. For safety purposes, people should be able to exit a data center quickly, bypassing the normal access requirements. In the case of a fire or a power outage, you don't want to risk the safety of your employees. Doors should have some sort of panic bar that can force them open in the case of an emergency. Of course, the use of a panic bar needs to be logged. If, due to design, your data center has doors that go to the outside of the building, they should be emergency exit doors only. They should have no key or door knob on the outside. Such exit doors need to be monitored by closed circuit cameras. If you have data centers in foreign countries, I recommend checking for these types of issues when performing your on-site security reviews. From a humanistic standpoint, it would be a tragedy for somebody to die in a data center because they could not get out in case of a fire or other emergency. From a business standpoint, it would cause a potential public relations nightmare as well.

Servers that reside in a data center should be in locked server cabinets. Control access to the server cabinets tightly. Individuals should only be given access to the cabinets that contain servers on which they are supposed to perform work. I know firsthand that computer engineers are curious people by nature. If nothing else, you want to stop the inquisitive from accessing systems that they do not have a business need to touch. The walls of a server room should go all the way up to the ceiling, slab to slab. If there is a space for a drop ceiling, an intruder could use that to climb over the wall, bypassing security measures to gain access to the data center.

Install cameras on all entrances and exits to your company's data centers. Maintain the images for a period of time that is long enough to be used for an investigation, if needed. Some cameras are motion activated, only taking continuous pictures if somebody enters its field of view. Some cameras are fixed, while other can be remotely rotated, allowing the operator to change their view. The recordings can also be saved to a computer hard drive, which has much greater storage capacity than VHS tapes. You could always archive older camera images to CD or other removable media to allow for even longer retention periods.

KEEP THE LIGHTS ON

While perhaps not purely a defense-in-depth issue from a confidentiality standpoint, there are availability issues that need to be considered for your electronic assets. Make sure your servers and mainframes have a reliable source of clean electricity. Since most computers don't react well to spikes, they should be plugged into surge suppressors that provide protection against electrical surges. If there is a loss of main power, you need to have a plan to either continue working or at a minimum permit your system to be turned off in a controlled manner. An abrupt loss of power can cause serious issues to computer systems. Many data centers and server rooms will have some kind of backup power source. This can consist of battery backup or on-site generators.

Secondary on-site power sources need to be sized properly. A common mistake is to size on-site power for when a data center first opens and then not take expansion into consideration. What was initially an hour of battery backup may only turn out to be 20 minutes. Can you safely turn off all the computers in your server room in that amount of time? Emergency power is no different than network bandwidth. As you add systems and increase usage, you need to ensure that you have the capacity to handle the extra load. If the goal is to keep the systems going in the event of main power loss, on-site generators will likely be the answer. Many such generators are powered by diesel fuel. This means that there will be anywhere from several hundred to several thousand gallons of diesel fuel on-site in storage tanks. The local fire department or even local city ordinance may place limits on how much diesel fuel you can maintain on-site. The concern there is the risk of having a massive fuel source in the case of a fire. Calculate the amount of electricity needed to run your systems with your on-site power source. This will determine the size and number of generators that you need. Remember, generators fail too—don't buy just one massive generator. You also need to calculate the rate of fuel consumption to determine how long the data center can operate with on-site emergency power. In the event of an emergency, you may not be on the priority list for additional fuel. Government agencies and hospitals generally take precedence, regardless of the wording of any fuel contracts that you might have. The actual physical protection of the fuel tanks themselves is also important. They should be housed in a location that protects them from being damaged or vandalized. As much as I hate to state the obvious, cigarette smoking should be strongly discouraged around fuel tanks.

Well-placed bollards by the entrances of your company's facilities will also offer a degree of protection. A bollard is a short vertical post, a series of which, when strategically positioned, can provide protection against out-of-control or ill-intentioned vehicles. This is not only important for data centers, but also for administrative offices, government buildings, and other at-risk facilities. The use of bollards is becoming more common around the world to deter vehicle-based terrorist actions from getting too close to buildings.

For banks, the security of ATM machines, while minimizing the inconvenience to your customers, is a big concern. Criminals are resorting to pulling ATM machines right out of the walls by using heavy chains and pick-up trucks. Some customers may also feel "exposed" by accessing an ATM that's located out in the open. Some companies have placed their ATM machines in a front foyer. This allows customers to access them even when the bank itself is closed. Consider having the doors to the foyer key-card controlled, with your customers' ATM card unlocking the door. Since customers using the ATM machines will have a card anyway, they'll already have the key. This will offer a degree of protection for your customers, as well as your ATM machines. Such a measure will also provide protection from the elements, something that your customers will appreciate, and that may reduce maintenance costs on your ATM machines.

SOCIAL ENGINEERING

Aside from technical controls and physical controls, the weakest link in the overall security chain is often people. Social engineering is a non-technical method many hackers use to gain unauthorized access into your company's systems. I have personally been allowed access into numerous "secure" facilities by good-natured employees holding the door open for me. You'd be surprised how helpful people are when you are dressed professionally, or have your hands full. Most will be all too happy to hold the door open for you. While I won't mention the company by name, kudos to the security director who challenged me as I approached an exit-only door to his data center facility. Well done, Kim.

For many publicly traded companies, the names of their senior executives are public knowledge. Employees are generally very helpful when they get a call from somebody claiming to be calling from the office of the CEO, or some other executive-level employee. Another common type of social engineering is to call an employee and claim to be from technical support. Again, the would-be hacker will likely be given all types of information, which can include an employee's username and password. An absolute no-win situation is when an employee gives sensitive information out to somebody claiming to be conducting a security audit of your company. If the person is a hacker, they have just received the data they need to try to gain access into your network. If the person really is from the company that is performing a security audit, receiving sensitive information on the phone without some sort of verification of their identity will likely result in a negative audit finding.

TRAINING AND AWARENESS

The best tools to combat social engineering are training and awareness. Employees should be told not to allow people into the building who they don't personally know by sight. Depending on the nature of a particular building, employees should be encouraged to challenge people they don't know who are inside of the facility. Most authorized visitors are issued badges to wear, and may be required to be escorted by an employee at all times. A word of caution here: Please be sure to take the welfare and safety of your employees into account when encouraging them to challenge people that may be in the facility without proper authorization.

Companies should have an established security and awareness program. Security should be part of the new hire orientation process, as well as part of an ongoing training for all employees. The training and awareness programs should be iterative, adapting to remain current with changes in both regulations and technology. Your employees need to have regular training to be aware of changes and requirements specific to security and data handling. This would, of course, also apply to engineers, security personnel, auditors, and compliance officers.

With all of the multiple layers of defense we've just discussed, you'd certainly want to know who is accessing your computer systems, as well as verifying that they are actually allowed to do so. Authentication and authorization are two very important tools that help you do just that.

CHAPTER 4

AUTHENTICATION AND AUTHORIZATION

While largely overlooked in most governmental regulations mandating the protection of sensitive data, authentication and authorization are arguably two of the most important weapons in the overall data privacy arsenal. Having well-thought-out and effective authentication and authorization controls will go a long way in protecting the privacy of sensitive data. Conversely, if done improperly, it can be one of your network's most serious security exposures. Many experts in the field of data privacy tout the strengths of encryption. While certainly important, its effectiveness is greatly reduced, and even eliminated, without proper authentication and authorizations controls. It is also the reason why, in any organization, the most sensitive data is often considered to be logon credentials.

If hackers can access your logon credentials, not only can they access what you can access and see what you can see, but in many cases they can perform such activities masquerading as you. So, when looking at what data your company needs to protect, remember the information that comprises your authentication and authorization controls. It is also a system that needs to be methodically planned out. One of the most serious security issues in many organizations are poor access controls. It is important not to give out the keys to the kingdom. Let's look at the differences between the two terms as well as some widely used industry tools that make the most of the two critical security components.

AUTHENTICATION

Authentication is the act of ensuring that people are who they say they are. There are three different types, or factors, of authentication. They are: what you know, what you have, and what you are.

1. What you know:
    a. Passwords
    b. Pass phrases
    c. Out of wallet questions (e.g., what is your grandmother's maiden name)
    d. Access codes
    e. PINs
2. What you have:
    a. Secure ID/Fob
    b. Electronic key card
    c. Brass key
    d. Passwords or pass phrases (once they are written down.)

I have placed passwords and pass phrases under "What you have" to illustrate an important point. Many people will write down their passwords in case they forget them. It is not unusual to see passwords taped to computer monitors, or to the back of laptops. Such practices obviously negate their effectiveness and are a major security concern. The millions that your company spent on encryption would be thwarted by such a practice.

3. What you are: (biometrics)
    a. Finger prints
    b. Palm prints
    c. Voice prints
    d. Retina scan
    e. Palm vein pattern*

BIOMETRIC AUTHENTICATION

Biometrics is considered a very strong authentication method because it is very difficult to fake somebody's fingerprints or retina pattern. However, as with any form of security control, nothing is foolproof. For example, while it is true that no two people have the exact same fingerprints, that doesn't mean it's impossible to foil fingerprint biometrics. When we touch a surface with our hands, we leave a residue called a latent fingerprint. Most of us have heard law enforcement use terms such as "dusting for prints." They are using powder to highlight the latent fingerprints, and tape to lift them off and preserve them as evidence. Hackers can use the same techniques to steal somebody's fingerprints and attempt to foil a biometric system. When fingerprints are used as a

---

*More popular in Japan than in the U.S. or Europe

form of authentication, the pattern is stored in a database. The user's saved print is then compared against his or her fingerprint when they use the biometric system for authentication.

This is no different than a system comparing your stored password with the password you just typed in to ensure they match. This makes the protection of the database that stores the fingerprint data very important. While it is possible to change your password, you cannot change your fingerprints. If a user's fingerprint pattern file is stolen, it will forever invalidate that form of biometric authentication for them. This is something to consider when being asked to provide your fingerprints to work in industries such as law enforcement, education, health care, and the financial sector. While I am all in favor of strong background checks, there is a concern over the security of the biometric data applicants are providing.

While fingerprints cannot be changed, voice patterns can. Many companies are using text-based voice verification as a form of biometric authentication. The nice thing about this is that the text can be changed. It is then possible to protect a user if a voice pattern that was tied to a specific text is compromised. You simply have them submit another voice sample using a different text, akin to having a user change their password. So, while biometrics is a very strong authentication tool, it is most effective used in combination with one of the other factors.

TWO-FACTOR AUTHENTICATION

The best way to increase the effectiveness of authentication is to require two different types (or factors) for access. Buildings that employ biometrics to gain access to sensitive areas like server rooms generally also have guards who check IDs as well. So, not only would you have to copy my fingerprints, you would have to have a valid ID, and if I am personally known to the security guard, you would also have to look like me to get past them. It is also not uncommon for secure buildings to require users to enter a code on a keypad in addition to the fingerprint match. That would be an example of two-factor authentication, consisting of what you are and what you know.

For an extra level of security, there is the sally port method. A sally port consists of having an outer door and an inner door to the secure area. Only one set of doors can be opened at any one time. So you must be between the two doors and enter an additional authentication requirement such as your fingerprint to get past the inner doors. These areas are sometimes weight sensitive as a way to stop two people from trying to access the secure area at the same time.

Properly implemented, two-factor authentication is a very powerful tool to ensure a person's identity. However, beware of misuse and the false sense of security that they can give. A common thread throughout all security methods is that you need to be able to maintain control over the security systems in order to help ensure their effectiveness. Also remember that most security measures are merely tools. Depending on how they are implemented, they can either be a benefit for, or a detractor to, good security.

DEVICE AUTHENTICATION

Another tool in the authentication arsenal is that of device authentication, only allowing access from a previously identified computer. Depending on how it is implemented, device authentication can be a powerful tool to combat hacking. If a server accepts communications from another computer, have it only accept inputs from that particular computer. The computer's IP address and/or MAC address (the address of a computer's network card) would be pre-registered with the "target" computer as being able to accept inbound communications. Probably one of the most common implementations of this type of authentication is in the backup tape architecture. Backup servers will only accept incoming data from systems that have been pre-defined. Conversely, the client backup systems will only send their data to the pre-defined backup serer. This is done by using the backup software. Client software is loaded on the systems that send their data to be backed up. Server software is loaded on the system that will accept the data and write it to tape.

So, in addition to having to steal the account ID and password, the hacker would have to trick the server into believing they are coming from the correct computer as well. Obviously, you could broaden the list of predefined systems that a server will accept communications from so that it includes known support engineers. This would afford the same extra level of protection if the account of a support engineer was stolen. Again, the hacker would have to use the stolen account information from the support engineer's computer itself. While a hacker could try to trick the target computer into believing they are coming from the correct computer, this still adds another level of complexity to their effort to steal your company's data. That is what computer security is all about— making your systems more hack resistant. (Remember, there is no such thing as being hack proof.) Device authentication can also be used to restrict employees to only logging on to systems that they are assigned to. Your company may have situations where, due to the nature of the data contained on workstations, you want to prohibit employees from trying to log on to a co-worker's computer. An example would be sales-people that have their client contact lists on their computers.

Device authentication can also be used to protect your customers who have online accounts and conduct business over the Internet. Obvious examples would be online banking, and for people who access their medical or health insurance information over the Internet. However, this could also apply to online shopping as well. Whether you are Ebay, Amazon, Wal-Mart, or any company with a very large online customer base, device authentication is both effective and of low impact. Since most people generally use the Internet for personal use from the same home computer, restricting their access to that computer would be a strong anti-hacking tool. If legitimate users tried to access their accounts from a different computer, they could be prompted to provide some pre-defined out of wallet information, like their grandmother's maiden name. This would not be a major inconvenience for the consumer and, with the level of awareness of data breach and ID theft issues on the rise, most would appreciate being afforded the added level of protection.

CONTROL IS KEY

As is true with most security measures, control is a key aspect of effectiveness. Hand over the administration of security devices to a third party, and you risk compromising their protective value. Authentication is no different. Let me illustrate this by a common misuse of what is generally considered a strong authentication methodology, two-factor authentication.

One example of misuse consists of overseas outsourcing companies requiring two-factor authentication for their employees to log on to their workstations. The workstations are then used to access data on the U.S.-based companies that have outsourced work to them. Generally speaking, in such scenarios the two-factor authentication will consist of a thumb print and a password. However, just as passwords can be shared, employees can always have a co-worker press their thumb on their workstation so that they can access the data. This type of two-factor authentication was intended to thwart hackers who have stolen laptops. In this situation, biometric authentication is quite effective to protect laptops due to their mobility. But the method isn't as effective for workstations, which are not supposed to be taken out of the work environment. It offers no protection against co-workers sharing accounts if they are willing to share passwords and other credentials.

Many overseas companies advertise the fact that they use two-factor authentication as a way to demonstrate that they are security conscious. In most overseas outsourcing situations, all security at the non-U.S. facility is managed by the local company. The U.S.-based company has effectively turned over the security oversight of the overseas company accessing its network to the company itself. When security is outsourced to the service provider themselves, its effectiveness is weakened at best and possibly negated altogether.

The domestic company has no idea how the security is being managed, logged, enforced, or audited. The company has been told it exists and assured that it is safe. Many just leave it at that. Separation of duties would dictate that you should not outsource access to your company's assets and the security oversight to the same entity. Do you think they have a strong motivation to report egregious security violations to you? They are not going to want to jeopardize their business relationship by letting you know that one of their employees was sharing access with a co-worker or viewing sensitive data they had no business need to see. A general rule of thumb is that whoever has access to a device can circumvent any of its security measures. Turning over total administration of authentication to a third-party service provider, whether domestic or overseas, is placing the resources they have access to at risk. Maintain at least part of the authentication process in-house. For example, permit service providers to log on to their workstations locally, but manage access to your company's servers in-house.

AUTHENTICATION FOR MOBILE EMPLOYEES

Now let's look at the proper uses of two-factor authentication. I have already discussed two-factor authentication as a means to control physical access. Another common use is to enable remote or mobile users to access their company's network from a laptop. For this type of remote access, the type of two-factor authentication generally used consists of a username/password and a physical token such as an RSA Secure ID/Fob whose numbers change every 60 seconds. This not only provides for strong security, but is actually easier for the average end-user to deal with than a long and complex password.

However, for this model to be effective, it is assumed that the company is managing its own two-factor authentication infrastructure. Generally, it would consist of servers that check the code that the remote user would enter off of their ID/fobs, as well as the servers that maintain the username/password files. This type of system is not only effective to give remote employees access; it can also be used to grant temporary (on-demand) access to non-employee support personnel. Access granted by an ID/fob can be turned on and off, thus granting support personnel access in the event of a production emergency. This is easily done since ID/fobs all have serial numbers on them. So, it would be a matter of maintaining a database of users, and the specific ID/fob that they've been issued. The individual ID/fob could then be easily enabled as required.

This effectively restricts the time that non-employees have remote access to your systems, reducing your company's security exposure.

INTERNET-BASED AUTHENTICATION

As mentioned, security is compromised when you don't manage the actual tools that are used. Another example of this is with services that provide remote access to company computers for your people. There are service providers that sell the ability to allow your employees to access company issued workstations or other computers remotely using their infrastructure. This is generally used by companies that don't want to maintain their own remote-access infrastructure, due to a lack of either funding or technical expertise. Generally, your employees would be using the provider's network as a stopping point, hitting the remote access server, which then redirects the user to your company's network. Here are some questions to consider before making use of such services:

- Is the data encrypted as it is being transmitted from your employee's computer to the provider's network, and on to your company's remote system?
- Does any of the data being transmitted reside on your provider's systems? If so, how it is protected?
- Is any data co-mingled with data from their other customers?
- Who at the service provider would have access to your company's data?

In a nutshell, this type of remote access is about as secure as using an Internet Web mail-type account to send/receive sensitive data via e-mail instead of your company's own e-mail infrastructure. Many times in such a scenario, the third party also performs at least part of the authentication. So, not only is your company's data at risk at the provider's network, but all or part of the authentication controls have been turned over to them as well.

COMPLEX PASSWORDS

Another hard balancing act is to reconcile the security benefits of long passwords with the impact on your end-users trying to remember them. There are problems with requiring end-users (humans) to use long and complex passwords. We have a bad habit of writing down complex passwords, generally right by our computer monitors, or taped to the bottom of our laptops. This obviously impacts the effectiveness of the password. We also forget passwords, which results in system lock-outs and thus requires a procedure in place to support unlocking the computers. Computers that automatically unlock themselves are considered more susceptible to password-cracking attacks such as "dictionary" or brute force attacks. Requiring a system administrator to unlock an account does provide for stronger security, but it is also more expensive. Of course, long and complex passwords aggravate that situation.

Two-factor authentication is one way to help resolve this: requiring a less complex password, with a second factor such as the ID/fob mentioned above. There are many examples of this in everyday life. Some such examples include bank ATM machines, credit or debit card purchases at the gas pump, and debit card purchases at any number of retailers. All require both the card and knowledge of a PIN. There's also a single-factor alternative to complex passwords: pass phrases. Allow users to pick a long phrase, something that is both hard to hack, but easy for them to remember. A pass phrase can be just about anything. It can be a line from a movie, part of a favorite song, a phrase used by your grandmother when you were a child, etc. My grandmother used to have a saying when she was looking for something that wound up being in plain sight all the time. She would say, "If it were a snake, it would have bit me." That pass phrase would be very difficult for a hacker to crack, and is a lot easier for me to memorize than T5#udi31Afer4. Making slight alterations to pass phrases make them even harder to hack. For instance, "Which came **1st**, the chicken **0**r the egg**!**" as a variant to, "Which came **first**, the chicken **or** the egg**?**"

I often preach that security doesn't have to be expensive or hard to implement. Allowing pass phrases instead of complex passwords is an example of that. Not that complex passwords don't have a place. Complexity works well when it comes to system passwords and application passwords. In other words, instances where only a computer has to enter in the password and not the end-user—such is the case, for example, with service accounts used by applications. Since computers don't forget passwords like we poor humans do, it is possible to benefit from the security afforded by a long and complex password, without the overhead created when people forget them.

SINGLE SIGN-ON

Some companies have opted to use what is known as single sign-on. This allows an end-user to enter in their user name and password once to the network and access all additional authorized enterprise resources. Having to sign on only one time is certainly easier for the end-user. It also saves them from having to remember different passwords to the various systems that they have access to enterprise-wide. It would reduce the instances of forgotten passwords. On the down side, if a password is compromised, the hacker would be able to access all authorized systems. From a technical standpoint, different computing platforms often have unique and competing password requirements. Finding a single password construct that is acceptable to the various systems may be a challenge.

AUTOMATED PASSWORD RESET

Having engineers whose primary tasks are to unlock user accounts and to issue one-time passwords to end-users who have forgotten their passwords can be a real cost to companies. Some organizations have opted to deploy automated password reset systems in an effort to realize some cost savings. Such applications allow end-users to authenticate themselves by answering a couple out of wallet questions, such as, "What's your childhood dog's name?" Once they've been authenticated, end-users can unlock their own accounts and reset their own passwords. Security of the server that houses the end-users' out of wallet responses is very important. If compromised, a hacker could impersonate any user that was registered on the system.

AUTHORIZATION

Once you know who somebody is (authentication), next comes verifying that this person is permitted to access the intended systems and data (authorization). Some of the most common errors made in this area include default and shared accounts, as well as giving people more access than is required for them to complete their job functions.

DEFAULT ACCOUNTS, AND SHARED ACCOUNTS

Certain computing and network-type devices are shipped from the manufacturer with default accounts and passwords. Such default accounts should be changed or deleted before the devices are ever placed into production. Shared accounts are ones that give access to a computer, a network device, or a data set, and are shared among two or more individuals. The more people that share a single account, the harder it is to hold any one individual accountable for any misdeed committed by that access. It makes it harder to hold a single person accountable if the shared account is used for commit acts such of fraud, embezzlement, hacking, viewing inappropriate Web sites, etc. It places the specter of suspicion on everybody that uses the shared account. It also complicates any personnel actions that would normally be taken for such infractions, and can even complicate legal issues if the infraction were to rise to the level of a criminal act.

LEAST PRIVILEGED ACCESS

Another common mistake is granting more access than is needed. One of the cornerstones of information security is that of "least privileged accesses," or granting only the level of access needed to perform the requirements of the job. It is certainly easier to grant people high levels of access, because then you know that they'll have the capabilities to perform the work on a given system. I actually call it "lazy engineering" to give somebody Administrator Rights (Windows) or Root (Unix/Linux), because it is easier than finding out what level of access they really require. It takes thought, planning, and a level of effort to understand what amount of access is actually necessary. Many service providers will claim that they need highly privileged account access to systems on your network in order to perform their duties. While in some cases this may be true, most often it is lazy engineering on their part. Giving out high levels of privileged access carries other risks as well. With the right level of access, an engineer can disable or alter any security features that may be active on a given system. In short, they can cover their tracks.

I mentioned earlier in the book the theory of the CIA triad (confidentiality, integrity, and availability). Giving people higher levels of access than is needed can cause availability concerns as well. End-users with administrator rights can inadvertently crash their systems. They can download unsafe or pirated software, accidentally disable anti-virus or personal firewalls, etc. Your company can be held criminally liable for software piracy committed on your computers by your employees. Any computer engineer who has provided first level support knows that an end-user has more ability to break a system than they have to fix one.

REVIEW ACCESS REQUIREMENTS

Other important aspects of authorization are accountability and review. Know who within your company is empowered to grant access to systems. Depending on the nature of the company, it can be the owner of the data, the administrator of the given system, or a more centralized identity management group whose charter is IT security. Another common error is that once access is granted, it is not reviewed regularly. Access should be reviewed routinely to verify that it is still appropriate. The frequency of such reviews would be dependent on several factors. Privileged accounts should be reviewed more often than lower-level accounts. Individuals who change jobs within your company should have their access adjusted to meet the needs of their new position.

Separated employees can be a major security risk. You do not want former employees to have access to your computer network. Consider the risk of a newly fired employee with remote access to your company's network. Similar procedures would also apply to temporary and seasonal employees as well as contractors and vendors who have access to your systems. The process of removing access when employees leave a company, or the off-boarding process as I call it, needs to be as formal as when bringing a new employee into the organization. All of their user accounts should be deleted, ID/fobs cancelled, electronic key card access terminated, and biometric access removed. As you can see, the list can be very long, and does need to be comprehensive.

An area often overlooked is notifying security personnel that monitor access at the entrance to your facility. They will likely recognize the dismissed employee, and if they have not been told that the employee has been fired, will very likely grant them access into the building. I find it interesting that while most companies do not have a well-documented set of procedures to remove an employee's system access when they leave a company, they sure have a solid process to remove them from payroll and any benefits that they might have been receiving as an employee.

While it is not uncommon for former employees to have active user accounts years after they have left a company, I have never heard of a situation where they have continued to get paid during that time. There are two lessons to be learned from this. The first one is that since there is an obvious financial impact in continuing to pay an employee's salary and benefits after they've left the company. That is why most companies have a mature, well-documented procedure for financially off-boarding employees. The financial impact of not deleting system access is less obvious, and is only costly if the former employee tries to exploit the access for financial gain or just to cause harm. Hence, the lack of a well-documented process. The second lesson is that there's a synergy here. The process to remove a former employee's system access can be integrated into the existing financial off-boarding process. You do not have to re-invent the wheel, just make some enhancements.

USER PROFILES VERSUS GROUP PROFILES

Reviewing user access rights can be a daunting task. The issue gets more complicated as companies grow in size. End-user account administration can become a nightmare as the number of employees reaches the tens of thousands. It's very difficult for computer engineers to properly administer such a large number of individual user accounts. If a company has a lot of turnover, or employees that frequently change jobs within the organization, the task gets even more difficult. Managers are often tasked with verifying the access of the individuals on their team on a recurring basis. If you manage a large team with access to a wide range of systems, this too can be a near-impossible task to perform with any degree of accuracy.

The implementation of user groups can go a long way to resolving this problem. If as a manager you have a team of 100 users that perform five different tasks at a high level,(finance, sales, marketing, analytics, etc.), there may be an opportunity to create five group profiles. So, instead of having to review 100 distinct user accounts, you would just have to ensure that the five profiles are still accurate, and that all individuals that are in the various groups are still on your team. It is certainly easier to place a new employee into a pre-defined group rather than trying to remember each system they may need access to.

KERBEROS

Companies often wrestle with how to control the access to their computer assets. Then there is the issue of protecting usernames and passwords as they are being transmitted across your network as well. There are tools available on the market today that provide comprehensive solutions. Kerberos is one such tool. Created by the Massachusetts Institute of Technology, Kerberos is an effective network authentication tool. It was designed to provide strong authentication for client/server applications by using a technology known as secret-key cryptography. Secret-key cryptography, also known as symmetric cryptography, uses the same encryption key to both encrypt and decrypt data. A client/server application model consists of an end-user's computer, the client, accessing an application on a different computer, the server. Most client/server applications rely on the client program to be "honest" about the identity of the user who is using it. Some other applications rely on the client to restrict its activities to those it is allowed to do, and in most cases with no other enforcement by the server.

Kerberos uses strong encryption so that a client can prove its identity to a server (and vice versa) across an insecure network connection. After a client and server have both used Kerberos to prove their respective identities, they can also encrypt all of their communications to ensure privacy and data integrity as they go about their business. In Kerberos, all authentications take place between clients and servers. The implementation consists of a Kerberos server, generally referred to as a Key Distribution Center or KDC. The KDC has two functions. It acts as an Authentication Server (AS), which authenticates both of the principals, the client and server, via a pre-exchanged secret-key. The second function of the KDC server is that of a Ticket Granting Server or TGS. The TGS provides a means to securely establish a trusted relationship between the two principals, those being the client (workstation) and the server.

When a user first authenticates to Kerberos, he communicates with the Authentication Service on the KDC to get a Ticket Granting Ticket. This ticket is encrypted with the user's password. From that point, when the user wants to communicate with a Kerberized service, he uses the Ticket Granting Ticket to talk to the Ticket Granting Service. The Ticket Granting Service verifies the user's identity using the Ticket Granting Ticket and issues a ticket for the desired service on a given server. Once authenticated, a user doesn't have to enter in their password every time they wish to connect to a Kerberized service or keep a copy of their password around.

There are security issues related to Kerberos. The security of the Key Distribution Server is very critical. If the KDC is compromised, the hacker can potentially exploit access to all Kerberized servers. If a client system is compromised, a hacker could access servers that the end-user had access to. If security engineers are alerted to the fact that a particular client has been compromised, they can quickly invalidate the associated Kerberos ticket. This will in effect stop the hacker from using compromised system to access any of the client's Kerberized server access.

Like any other piece of security software or hardware, Kerberos is a tool. It takes skilled people to properly administer it, and it should be audited regularly. No security solution is a substitute for the vigilance of skilled security professionals. They are to be thought of as an augmentation and not as a substitution. For more information on Kerberos, go to http://web.mit.edu/kerberos/.

A common theme throughout information security, and hence throughout this book, is the effective use of multiple layers of security to provide the most effective levels of protection. Knowing who is accessing your company's resources, and ensuring that they are only given the level of access that they truly need, are the cornerstones of authentication and authorization. This becomes even more of a challenge when your workforce itself is mobile.

CHAPTER 5

SECURITY AND THE MOBILE EMPLOYEE

The era of the mobile employee has allowed those who travel extensively for work to be more productive. Salespeople, executives, and other professionals that have to travel for work now have the ability to stay connected to their company's network from just about anywhere. Many hotels now provide high speed Internet access right in their rooms. Most major metropolitan areas have Internet cafés allowing the traveler to work while eating lunch or having a cup of coffee. It is also common today to see people working on their laptops when flying on airplanes, or taking mass transit such as a subway. This kind of flexibility, while allowing for great productivity, does carry numerous security concerns.

It is possible for the employee on the go to remain protective while still not sacrificing security. Again, security and productivity are not competing forces in the workplace. Just like many of the other issues discussed in this book, it takes a degree of planning of resources, commitment, and a level of awareness. For the mobile employee, security can even be an awareness of your surroundings. The issues to consider for the mobile user go beyond whether to use a virtual private network (VPN) or a modem to connect to your company's network. There's also the protection of the data on the mobile device itself, as well as ensuring that sensitive data is not either seen or overheard by those around you.

Let's start off by concentrating on the security issues that companies face when their employees are connecting to their network over the Internet while traveling. There are three typical ways for the mobile employee to remotely connect to their company's network. They include a modem, a company owned and managed virtual private network (VPN), and a third party's VPN.

MODEMS

Modems are not only slow, but most are also very insecure. Standard modems transmit data unencrypted, thereby placing your information at risk. They also transmit data in an analog, rather than digital, fashion—just like normal phone lines. This causes a problem because firewalls are designed to inspect digital transmissions. A modem will therefore bypass a company's firewall, and if the transmission is compromised, the hacker will bypass the firewall as well. A well-known fictional compromise of a network using a modem was in the 1983 movie released by MGM called *War Games*. While admittedly done in a Hollywood fashion, it is a good illustration of how a hacker can use a modem to bypass normal perimeter security controls. Another concern are the backdoors that developers often place in the applications that they write. While they are sometimes referred to as maintenance hooks, a backdoor is a backdoor "Joshua." Since modems operate "out of band" using analog instead of digital, sometimes they are considered a tool of last resort for remote support engineers trying to resolve a serious system problem. They are also a low-cost solution to allow for engineering support of stand-alone servers in remote locations.

If the decision has been made to use modems, there are steps you can take to protect your data as well the rest of your network. There are modems that offer security features such as strong user authentication and encryption for data while in transit. Bear in mind that utilizing encryption will add overhead and subsequently slow things down. It will take even more time to transmit encrypted data over a modem. Modems can also be configured to dial the caller back. This is a way to try and foil the hacker who is trying to impersonate a legitimate remote user. If the number called isn't that of your support engineer or employee, watch out.

Modems are sometimes used to send out information, such as an alert in the event of some kind of system failure. It is possible to configure modems to dial out only, and not accept any incoming calls. Some models of modems, in addition to offering security features, can also accommodate multiple users at the same time. While this will reduce the cost of having to purchase a modem for each remote user, keep in mind the performance issue. Modems still operate over phone lines, and hence are very slow. Performance that would be bad enough with one user would only get worse with two or more simultaneous users.

The actual placement of modems is also an important security concern. Since a server that has a modem attached to it is more susceptible to being hacked, separate it from the rest of your network. If the system is a stand-alone server that isn't attached to the rest of your company's network, that's one thing. However, if the server is attached to the rest of your company's network, you should place it in a DMZ. (DMZs are discussed in Chapter 2.)

Modems can also be used on an as-needed basis to provide technical support. In such cases, an effective security control is to leave the modem unplugged until such support is needed. The cautionary word here is that you are now placing the responsibility for making sure a major security hole does not develop on the assumption that nobody will forget to unplug the modem once the issue has been resolved. If such a support scenario is being used, have a formal procedural checklist that includes unplugging the modem as part of the overall process.

VIRTUAL PRIVATE NETWORKS (VPNS)

A VPN encrypts data while in transit, and unlike a modem that will "answer" if its number is dialed, a VPN is normally configured to require strong two-factor authentication. A common authentication method with many VPN solutions is to require the mobile worker to enter in a password, as well as a PIN from a physical token known as an ID/fob. This would require the would-be hacker to not only steal the ID/fob, but to know the user's account name and password. The best architecture for a VPN solution is for the VPN server to reside in your company's DMZ. This would allow the server to accept encrypted data transmissions. The VPN tunnel would terminate at the server, allowing decrypted traffic to proceed into the internal network. The benefit of this type of architecture is that the company's intrusion detection systems (IDS) can inspect the transmission. A common misconception with encryption is that it always adds to security. Encryption, like anything else, is a tool, and if misused can actually be a security hazard. Network-based intrusion detection systems (IDS) sensors inspect data as it traverses a network, looking for inappropriate transmissions. What is considered inappropriate is generally defined by the security engineers configuring them. They generally consist of known bad items (signatures) or traffic that is out of the ordinary (anomalies). IDS sensors cannot inspect data that is encrypted because the only thing they see is encrypted data, also known as cipher-text.

If maintaining an internal VPN solution is not in your company's business model, due to either cost restrictions or a lack of internal technical expertise, there are other options. There are companies that offer VPN services. If you are considering this, there are some security issues to consider:

- Will the data that your employees transmit reside on your VPN provider's network?
- If so, how will they secure it?
- Would your data potentially be exposed to the employees of the VPN provider?

- How secure is their network?
- Would a compromise of their network put your company at risk?
- Would other companies using their VPN service potentially have access to your data?

Remember, going to an outside service provider should not mean lowering your security standards to meet those of the third party. If they can't protect your data to a level that you're comfortable with, seek out another provider that can. One of the great things about living in the United States is that we have choices. In most cases, there are likely to be numerous companies offering the same service. Seek out the best service, which includes security, for the most competitive prices.

There's another scenario. Say a company that you've contracted with to provide a service, which requires them to have remote access into your network, wants to use their own VPN solution. In most instances, this would entail having an encrypted VPN tunnel originate at the other company's network and go all the way into your network to the system they require access to. This is yet another example of where encryption can be a security hazard. Your service provider could be doing anything along that encrypted VPN tunnel connecting the two networks with a high degree of secrecy. That's secrecy from you, since such a setup would bypass most normal security controls that companies have in place. Under no circumstances allow a third party to have an encrypted tunnel right into the interior of your network. If the vendor insists upon it, don't do business with them.

DATA ON LAPTOPS

Beyond protecting data in transit, there is also the issue of protecting the laptop itself. Numerous companies, such as PointSec and Safeguard, offer hard drive encryption. This protects the data on laptops if they are stolen. A word of caution here: Hard-drive encryption is not the same as file-level encryption. Once the laptop is turned on, and the end-user bypasses the hard drive application's username/password challenge, it does not offer any protection, because it is designed to protect data on a laptop that has been stolen. Hard drive encryption solutions encrypt every sector of a hard drive, each with its own encryption key pair. Such a solution is generally considered very difficult to thwart due to the sheer number of encryption key pairs to be hacked.

There is also a technology called removable media encryption (RME). Once installed on a laptop, it will encrypt data that is copied to a CD or a thumb drive. This will make the data unreadable to any computer that is not a part of the network employing the RME solution.

A low-tech hacking technique that the mobile worker needs to be aware of is known as shoulder surfing, or curious people trying to see what's on your computer screen. Airplanes, subways, and Internet cafés are busy places, and you can't always know who may be trying to see what's on your laptop. There are filters that you can place over your laptop's screen to protect from shoulder surfers. These filters obscure the data on your screen unless you're looking straight at it. So, while not perfect, it will foil the person sitting beside you on the airplane trying to read your data at an angle. An additional security measure would be to not conduct sensitive business on laptops in crowded public places. Be aware of your surroundings; the person sitting behind you at the coffee house could be stealing data from your laptop with their cell phone camera.

PROTECTION OF LAPTOPS WHILE TRAVELING

Employees traveling with their laptops face a number of security concerns. First, use common sense. Countless laptops have been stolen right out of unlocked cars, hotel rooms, and from unattended backpacks. When I travel on business, I go right from my house to the airport with no intermediate stops. I've just eliminated the risk of my laptop being stolen because I've left it unattended in my car. While traveling, the laptop is either with me or locked in a safe. When choosing a hotel, ask if they have a safe in the room large enough to hold a laptop. Some older hotels have safes only large enough to hold cash and jewelry. Some will have safe deposits boxes available for their guests as well.

Remember that thieves know the hotels that are frequented by business travelers and executives. Many hotel employees have keys to our hotel rooms, including bell boys, cleaning staff, and others. Leaving a laptop unprotected in your hotel room is just asking for trouble. Lock it up, carry it with you, or leave the laptop at your office.

Laptops can also get stolen when you're passing through a security checkpoint at an airport. Thieves will take advantage of the level of confusion that exists in many airport security checkpoints to try and steal laptops from unsuspecting travelers. The best defense here is to first of all to only take your laptop with you if absolutely necessary. Secondly, be aware of your surroundings, and keep an eye on your laptop the best that you can as you're passing through the security checkpoint.

CELL PHONES AND PDAS

You see it all the time—people conducting business in public using their cell phones and PDAs. Some people have become so dependent on their Blackberry devices that the term "crackberry" has become a part of our cultural lexicon. The term is used to indicate an almost drug-like dependency. The truth is that such devices allow people to conduct business almost anywhere. They use wireless technology to make phone calls, as well as to send and receive e-mails. When you use a wireless-enabled device in a crowded public place, you have the risk of having your data stolen by hackers.

BLUETOOTH—BLUESNARFING—BLUEJACKING

Bluetooth is a wireless technology that is generally associated with personal devices such as PDAs and cell phones. Many wireless keyboards and mice also use Bluetooth. Since it's designed to be more of a personal solution, the effective range of Bluetooth is limited to about 10 meters for cell phones and PDAs, and about 100 meters for laptops. In the name of ease of use, many Bluetooth-enabled devices have a feature called "self-discovery." Locking onto another signal is popularly known as "Bluesnarfing." People will seek out other Bluetooth-enabled devices within their range limit. So, by Bluesnarfing, it is possible to steal information from other Bluetooth-enabled devices that are within range. If you're in a coffee shop, a high-rise office building, a subway system, or an airport you could be talking about a lot of devices. The Bluesnarfing hacker can steal information right off your PDA or cell phone as you're conducting business in a public place, or even from an adjoining floor of a multi-tenet office building. As opposed to Bluesnarfing, which is about stealing data, "Bluejacking" tries to send data to another Bluetooth-enabled cell phone or PDA.

The solution is simple. Set your Bluetooth device to "undiscoverable" as a way to combat either of these types of attacks.

BE AWARE OF YOUR SURROUNDINGS

As you are working on your Palm Pilot, Blackberry, or another other personal device, be aware of your surroundings. Sometimes, hacking is no more ingenious than someone peering over your shoulder to see the data on your display screen. The same word of caution applies to having that confidential conversation on your cell phone. Be aware of people who may be listening in on your conversations. Some people speak so loudly when talking on their cell phones, you can't help but hear their conversations. This is annoying as well as insecure. Also be aware that cell phones in general are not as secure as landline telephones are. If the telephone conservation involves discussing highly sensitive information, consider using a landline phone.

Many brands of PDAs can be password-enabled. While certainly not hack proof, utilizing a password will afford a certain level of protection.

If your company has a policy requiring that e-mails containing sensitive data be encrypted, ensure that is applied to e-mails sent by PDAs as well. There are third-party software providers that offer encryption solutions for PDAs. Blackberry's own Web site talks about an encryption solution for their PDA, utilizing strong algorithms such as 3-DES and AES.

The advent of the mobile workforce has allowed companies to realize higher levels of worker productivity. Keeping mobile data safe is just another challenge for the information security professional. Security is not the antithesis to productivity; when done properly, they actually go hand in hand.

CHAPTER 6

BUSINESS CONTINUITY PLANNING

Business Continuity Plans (BCP), Disaster Recovery Plans (DRP), and Continuation of Operations Plans (COOP), at the end of the day, all have a similar theme. In the event of a work interruption, minor or catastrophic, whether man-made or due to the forces of nature, does your company have a plan to keep the lights on and stay in business? This is not just an issue that is strictly for the computer engineers to handle. Asset loss can include a loss of electrical power, phone lines, and even an inability of employees to report for work due to an interruption in mass transit. Whatever the cause, a question to ask yourself is just how long can your company go without key assets, people, or property, before its very survival is in question.

For example, does your company have plans in place that will allow you to continue to operate in the event of the loss of an office building? What would you do if you lost your entire data center due to fire? If your answer is "I don't know," then your company risks going out of business if such an event occurs. If your answer is, "Sure, we have a plan, it was drawn up years ago by an employee that doesn't work here anymore, and it resides on some computer system somewhere," you are not much better off. The risks of not having effective contingency plans could mean that you temporarily close down for business. Costly for you and, even worse, beneficial for your competitors. Your customers will need to go somewhere for their needs.

Your company's business continuity plan (BCP) should be a living document. One that grows as your company grows. A plan that is both reviewed and rehearsed, at various levels, on a regular basis.

ACTS OF GOD AND MAN

Hurricanes, earthquakes, floods, and the like are natural occurrences and hence referred to as "acts of God." On the other hand, sabotage, terrorism, arson, and the like are acts of man. Both can physically devastate the facility in which your company's computer network is housed. Less permanent situations can also have a serious impact on your network's availability. Examples include a protest in front of your facility that blocks access to the building, or a power outage that deprives your computers of electricity. Table 6.1 lists many events that would have an impact, in some cases at a devastating level, on your company.

Are your prepared to deal with these types of occurrences? They are hard to predict and even harder to control, but they can be planned for. The goal of business continuity planning is to keep your business up and running in the event your company is hit by any of these types of situations. Do not make the mistake of assuming that your company could easily survive being out of business for a week or so with minimal financial impact. Remember, it is not only the loss of business while you're recovering from the event. You must also consider the fact that during that time, your customers were forced to go to your competitors. Some of them will not be coming back.

Table 6.1: Potentially Disastrous Events

Avalanche	Flood	Shooting
Severe Weather (heat, cold, blizzard, etc.)	Natural Gas Leak	Fuel Shortage (usually associated with a loss of main electrical power)
Biological Hazard	Heating, Ventilation, or Air Conditioning Failure	Bomb Threat
Civil Disorder	Hostage Situation	Kidnapping
Telecom Outage	Acts of Terrorism (9/11)	Theft
Robbery	Train Crash or Derailment	Lightning Strike
Computer/Software Failure, Virus or Destruction	Employee/Union strike	Acts of Vandalism
Pandemic	Picketing	Power Outage
Fire Damage	Water Damage	Radiological Hazard

BCP REGULATORY REQUIREMENTS

Would your company risk being in violation of any government laws or regulations if, due to a lack of a comprehensive BCP, you couldn't open your doors for a number of days? What would be the impact to a financial institution if it couldn't open for business, in violation of U.S. governmental regulations? This risk goes beyond just financial institutions. Consider the implications of not being able to produce documentation subpoenaed by a judge, or required as part of a Sarbanes-Oxley audit. I doubt either a judge or a government auditor would be satisfied with a response like, "We've lost the data, and don't have any backup tapes that we can restore from."

The United Kingdom recently published new guidelines for BCP. In December 2006, the British Standards Institute released a new independent standard, BS 25999. Prior to the introduction of BS25999, BCP professionals relied on BSI information security standard BS7799, which only peripherally addressed BCP to improve an organization's information security compliance. BS25999's applicability extends to organizations of all types, sizes, and missions, whether governmental or private, profit or non-profit, large or small, or industry sector. While this only applies to the United Kingdom, the data is very useful for non-British companies as well. After all, good due diligence is good due diligence.

In 2004, the United Kingdom enacted the Civil Contingencies Act, a statute that instructs all emergency services and local authorities to actively prepare and plan for emergencies. Local authorities also have the legal obligation under this act to actively lead promotion of business continuity practices in their geographical area.

In the United States, we have the Occupational Safety and Health Administration (OSHA), which enforces laws requiring that employers provide a safe working environment for their employees. Businesses, for example, are required to have an Emergency Action Plan in place to keep people safe in a disaster. There's also the Federal Emergency Management Administration (FEMA), which is chartered with bringing the resources of the federal government to bear to assist communities that have suffered disasters, such as hurricanes.

Preparing for natural disasters can, of course, be regionalized. For instance, if your company is off the coasts of Florida, it is more important to plan for hurricanes than it is for earthquakes. Whether it is earthquakes or hurricanes, if you have *all* of your company's assets housed in the same physical location, and if that facility is lost, you do not have any BCP plan. It is also important to understand that in the event of a disaster, employees may be faced with choosing between going to work, or staying at home to protect their families.

While often less devastating than acts of nature, acts of man can cause serious business interruptions as well. Malicious acts such as arson, a bomb threat, or a hostage situation can cause an interruption to business for various lengths of time. Depending on the extent of the damage of a fire, certain electronics may need to be replaced. The facility may be uninhabitable, and require major restoration work prior to employees returning to work.

A bomb threat, even a false one, will require that a building to be evacuated until the authorities can be certain that all is safe. A hostage situation will certainly stop all business-related functions in the effected area until the situation is resolved. While often not considered part of a BCP plan, your employees may need counseling after such a traumatic event.

Even if the facility itself is not damaged, but your employees can not access it due to issues such as interruptions in public transit, a parade in front of your building, a protest, etc., you need a plan for keeping the business up and running. For the latter, having employees who can work from home and function using remote access such as a virtual private network (VPN) would likely solve the problem for the short term. That would be as easy as ensuring key employees have a laptop, and your company has a functional VPN solution.

However, what if the facility itself is physically lost? The obvious answer is to have a second physical facility that can serve as a backup. Larger companies by their nature have multiple physical facilities, and with proper planning can build in redundancies that account for the loss of one building. There are also companies that will serve as your business's continuity site in the case of an emergency. Be careful, however; there are a lot of challenges with this type of solution. Most companies that offer BCP-type sites sell the service to multiple companies. So if the emergency that affected your business was widespread, you may find yourself vying for the limited space in the BCP site. Check the language in the contract with your BCP site provider and look for a guarantee of space if that is critical to your company's survival.

If your backup facility is to close to your primary one, the same event that compromised one can affect the other. For example, don't have both your primary and backup facilities served by the same power grid. If the grid is lost, both of your facilities will be affected. Even if the power grid is not totally gone but does suffer a significant loss of capacity, that could affect you as well. Hospitals and other emergency facilities are given priority in these types of situations. So, the lights don't have to be totally out for your company to be "in the dark." An example of this would be the rolling brown outs that California had several years ago. Another issue: Do not have both your primary and BCP facilities along the same earthquake fault line, or along the same coast line that could be affected by the same hurricane. In short, the same disaster, either natural or man-made, should not be able to affect both your primary and backup facilities. If they do, you would be well advised to take a hard look at your company's BCP plan.

HOT—WARM—COLD

If your company has multiple data centers, one could act as a backup if another were to go down. If not, going off-site would be required. From there, you would need to decide if you are going to utilize a cold site, warm site, or hot site. Each solution requires different levels of preparedness and cost. A cold site is usually just floor space, with none of the equipment in place that would ultimately be required in the event of a disaster. A warm site, on the other hand, will have much of the equipment in place, but will require a large amount of configuration and importing of data in order to make the facility functional as a backup facility. A hot site is supposed to be fully functional at all times, ready to be used if necessary. Each has a different cost structure. But keep in mind that with a hot site, you won't skip a beat, possibly saving you money in the long run.

CREATING A BUSINESS CONTINUITY PLAN

It's important to understand that you can't create a BCP in a vacuum. It will require input and cooperation from across your organization. For example, it is not sufficient to create a BCP for your department's server without involving other technology areas. Consider the situation of a department having a backup server to enable employees to continue working in the event the primary production server suffers an outage. While some may say that having a backup server is all that is needed to continue to function, consider some of the following issues.

- Has the backup server been maintained so that it mirrors production as closely as possible?
- Have software updates that have been made in production also been applied to the backup server, or is it several versions behind?
- Is the backup server of the same hardware level as the production server? If not, it may lack the capacity to function in the event of a production server outage.
- As new employees come into your department, are they given user accounts on the backup server similar to those on the production server? If not, they won't be able to access the backup server to perform their duties.

While there is more, of course, the point is that a BCP exercise needs to be company-wide, and can't function in departmentalized vacuums.

The first step in creating a BCP is to define your scope and objectives, identify possible interruptions, set timetables, identify required resources, gain management support, and identify your BCP team and team members' respective roles.

After that, perform a business impact analysis or BIA. Determine what your business's critical functions are, as well as financial and operational considerations, regulatory requirements, and threats to organizational reputation. Gather and analyze information to determine, for your critical functions, the recovery point objective, as well as the recovery time objective, if an "event" were to occur. Which functions must you recover first, and in what order? A recovery time objective is the maximum amount of time a certain function can be down before it is restored.

An effective business continuity plan requires a thorough understanding of your business activities. This includes things such as its critical functions and dependencies on things such as telephones, computer systems, physical facilities, network systems, and so forth. Having an in-depth understanding, and knowing the interdependencies of the parts, is critical to help determine what functions need to be restored first. For this, you'll always need an up-to-date equipment inventory. It is important for the people coordinating the recovery and response to know what was installed.

START WITH AN IT INVENTORY

To that end, start by doing a complete inventory of your network hardware resources. This includes routers, servers, switches, hubs, PBX switch boards, etc. When compiling your hardware list, make note of the manufacturer, the make and model, as well as any associated warranty information.

After you've compiled your hardware list, make a list of the software running on it. A software list would include operating systems and applications (database, e-mail, Web server, proprietary applications, client-side software such as Word, Excel, and more). For each piece of software, ensure that you have the current version number, as well as any warranty information. When compiling your software list, don't forget an up-to-date list of any patches, firmware updates, secure updates, etc. If you want your systems to act the same after an event, the software lists needs to be as exact as possible.

Compile, for both your hardware and your software, a complete list of suppliers. If you need to replace systems in a hurry, you'll need to know whom to call to gets things ordered in a hurry. This should also include any local electronic resources that may be more nimble than some of your regular suppliers.

It is not uncommon for companies to have both hardware and software that is several years old and no longer being made. A common industry term for such equipment is "end of life." Be sure that you've identified suppliers that carry your older equipment. If the original manufacturer doesn't stock it, older equipment is generally available on a secondary market. Make certain that you know who your local carriers are so that you can get equipment shipped to you as necessary. This is information you'll want to have before you need to enact your BCP. Some companies opt to require their primary suppliers to guarantee the availability of equipment that they purchased in the form of a Service Level Agreement (SLA), which is often written into the purchase contract. SLAs usually include language that requires suppliers to fix an outage within an agreed-upon timeframe. The SLA could require the vendor to replace a failed piece of equipment within a certain amount of time. SLAs of this nature are especially important for mission-critical servers, mainframe computers, routers, switches, and other network hardware. The higher the price tag, the greater the likelihood your vendor may work with you in agreeing to such SLAs. Negotiate disaster-recovery services with vendors when they are actively pursuing your business. It may be difficult to add them later, particularly if you're suffering from an outage.

It is important that your inventory of both hardware and software be kept current. Updating your BCP inventory should be integrated with the purchasing of new hardware and software. As new servers are purchased, or newer software versions are installed, make that information part of the BCP inventory if such systems need to be replaced. It is best if such a BCP equipment database is updated automatically in concert with the deployment of new hardware or software. And make sure you have off-site backup—it doesn't help if your BCP inventory database is lost in the same event that caused the system outage.

KEEP AN UPDATED LIST OF PERSONNEL

Beyond software and hardware, it is also critical to maintain an updated list of your company's personnel, as well as their contact information. This includes personal contact information where appropriate. Emergencies of a given scale can also come with a certain degree of confusion, and it's important to be able to ensure that your company's personnel can be accounted for. Knowing who is on vacation or out sick is important so they're not mis-identified as being unaccounted for in a damaged facility. This could expose emergency response personnel to unnecessary risk as they search for an employee who's vacationing in Hawaii. Consider having floor captains responsible for making sure that everybody safely exits the building as necessary. (Include at least one man and one woman so that restrooms can be checked.) Make certain to account for any employee with either physical limitations or medical conditions. Do you have a plan to get a wheelchair-bound employee safely out of your tenth floor office in the event of a building fire?

Personnel determined as being key players in the event a BCP needs to be initiated should be kept on a BCP access list. As with the equipment inventory, this list needs to be in a protected off-site location. It is common practice, for all personnel that are part of the BCP core team, to keep such a list at their homes.

In addition to internal key personnel and hardware and software manufacturers, you'll also need to have contact information for your telecommunication providers (voice/network), your ISP providers, and any other key vendors.

MAKE IT A COMPANYWIDE PLAN

The larger a company is, the more likely that a certain degree of departmentalization will occur. While this is unavoidable, having several disconnected BCPs is an almost certain recipe for failure. Individual departmental BCPs need to be consolidated into a master corporate BCP. These will aid in identifying any efficiencies of scale, as well as corporate priorities. If several departments share the same administrative building, it makes little sense for each of them to plan for their own backup facility in the event of an emergency. Another hard truth is that all departmental managers have their own feelings and opinions on how critical their areas are to the corporation and just where on the BCP priority list they should fall. As a result, these types of decisions need to be made at a very senior level on a centralized corporate basis.

Because businesses are so different, no one BCP will fit every company. You'll need to create a custom plan. Issues that need to be taken into consideration include the following. First, it is important to consider what precisely your goals are in the event that you need to go into a BCP mode. From a humanitarian standpoint, the first consideration should be the protection of human life. Secondly, you'll want to be able to resume operations, even if on a diminished basis, as soon as possible. To do this, you need to determine which operations need to be restored first. Depending on your business, it could be your Web site, your call center, or a major database system. A good way to determine what operations need to be restored first is to have a frank discussion about the impact to your company if certain functions are down for a given period of time. How long can they be down before your company risks losing customers, market share, and a loss of shareholder equity? Will an outage lasting more than a couple of days result in your company facing litigation or government fines? At what point does the very survival of your company come into question? Those are the criteria used to help identify which critical systems need to be restored, and how soon.

If an event does occur, do people know what to do, or is this knowledge just restricted to the team members who drew up the BCP? Would your night watchman know whom to contact if he discovered a water leak in your server room at 2:00 A.M.? What about your night janitorial staff? The point is, BCP information, especially initial response procedures, should be widely known and clearly posted. Such information would include the phone numbers of local emergency services, including police, fire, and paramedics. If your building has a facilities manager, or a local BCP first responder team, their contact information should be included in such a list as well.

Beyond the initial response after an event, you'll need to know what to do. Providing for the security of the damaged facility is important. In addition to the welfare of your employees and customers, you'll also want to protect your equipment as well as your data. Will you be able to determine who is an employee and who is a looter? Having a meeting area for employees in case of an emergency will help determine friend from foe. It will also help identify if any employees, who may be injured, are missing.

If the incident if serious enough, local employees need to notify the corporate BCP team, sometimes referred to as an Emergency Management Team (EMT). These are the people who can bring corporate resources to bear to handle events of a larger scale. They will need to assess the scope of the damages to determine appropriate next steps. Will employees need to be taken to an alternate site? Is it even possible to get to the alternate site? Such situations can be very stressful for your employees. Providing essentials such as food and water are also a part of a BCP. I've seen situations where damaged sites had no working restrooms. That is certainly a morale buster.

Once an initial assessment has been made, determine what needs to be purchased. Ensure that local management has sufficient funding authority to make emergency purchases. Don't let red tape cause a delay of several days when you're trying to recover from an event. Depending on its scale, the event that caused you to go into BCP mode will draw media attention. Know who is responsible for speaking to the media, as well as customers and employees. Who is going to make a statement to your shareholders?

After the initial dust settles, compile a complete list of damages so that you can respond as necessary. Know what to buy, who to call, and even whether or not your employees need to be relocated to an alternate site. This is where employees working out of their homes and connecting to the corporate network via a VPN can come in handy.

Bear in mind that the process of re-establishing critical functions entails more than just purchasing hardware and software. The new systems will need to be configured and tested to make certain that they function as expected. Have an agreed-upon criteria for what constitutes a successful test prior to clearing systems for production. You don't want to risk causing more problems by placing untested systems into production in a rush to get back to normal. Do not place unsecured systems into production to get back to work quicker. Hackers know that a company that is trying to cope with a BCP event is more vulnerable to attack. The volume of computer attacks against U.S. based companies spiked on September 11, 2001. Don't compound your BCP problems with a security breach. Beyond engaging your computer engineers, and depending on the nature of the damages, you could also need to rewire for power, network computer access (both LAN and WAN), and telephone service.

Once critical functions have been restored, it is important to assess the extent of the damages, and what needs to happen to return to a state of normalcy. A return to normalcy is not just limited to returning to your primary worksite and having all systems functioning properly. Consider the impact to your employees. Did any of them perform above and beyond the call of duty and deserve special recognition? Did the stress of the event impact your employees to an extent where professional assistance may be required? This is particularly relevant if the event included the loss of human life. Consider allowing for some additional paid time off for employees who were harried as a result of working through the BCP event. It is not uncommon for companies to experience a large amount of employee turnover in the aftermath of a serious event. Trying your best to minimize that is not only the right thing to do, it's also good business. Retention is cheaper than recruitment.

POST-DISASTER: REASSESS THE PLAN

Once operations return to normal, it's important to assess the effectiveness of how your company responded to an actual emergency. Business continuity planning is fine, but where the rubber meets the road is when it has to be put into use. It's important to determine what worked, what didn't, and in both cases, why. Keeping a running log of events throughout the entire business resumption process will help in performing a "lessons learned" exercise. BCPs can and should be adjusted as required.

It is very difficult if not impossible to anticipate every eventuality that may occur in a BCP. I doubt many of the companies housed in the Twin Towers had documented plans to recover from the attacks of 9/11. That attack not only wiped out equipment, but some companies lost a majority of their staffs as well. While trying to be comprehensive is important, understand that you can't foretell the future.

Your BCP should be a broad-based document, but it needs to provide enough detail to guide specific actions. It can't be a 50,000-foot view of your organization; that won't provide sufficient granularity. Remember that the best decisions are always well informed ones. Having complete information that is easily accessible will allow hard decisions to be made more easily in the event a company must invoke its BCP. Scrambling to gather information as the smoke is rising from the building is a recipe for disaster.

Disaster-recovery plans are complex and can take years to complete. If your BCP is an afterthought, your company will almost certainly have to scramble to recover from a system outage. Companies should have employees dedicated to working with the various departments to help them create their business continuity plans. Once written, it should be reviewed at least annually to ensure that it is kept current.

CHAPTER 7

HACKERS, SNOOPS, AND VIRUSES

Computer networks are under almost constant attack from hackers who are trying to cause harm or simple mischief. If that statement sounds a bit alarmist, consider how long your company would be in business if it were to take down all of its perimeter firewalls, even for just a couple of hours. In the Internet era, within a matter of minutes such news would be relayed to hackers around the globe.

Different people are motivated by different things, and hackers are no different. Some are merely curious and can be considered passive hackers or snoops. Active hackers on the other hand will cause some damage to your company's network if given the opportunity to do so. Whether it's to steal information, to corrupt it in order to prevent companies from using the data themselves, or even just to make systems temprorarily unavialbable, the hackers are out there. It may be for profit or it may be for bragging rights. Worse, it could be one of the most dangerous types of hacker, the hacker activist.

HACKER ACTIVISM (HACKTIVISM)

A hacker activist may feel justified in attacking your company's network for any number of reasons. In the mind of a hacker, this type of radical social justice is not only justified, but it is their moral obligation to punish a company doing something that, according to them, is wrong. This could include energy companies such as one of the big oil companies, pharmaceutical companies, automobile manufacturers, or large companies vilified in the press for not paying their employees enough or because the CEO makes too much money—the list goes on and on.

One of the biggest social issues of the day is man-made global warming. Any company deemed to have too large of a carbon footprint could be a target. Just having deep pockets could make your company a target for hackers with a "Robin Hood" syndrome—take from the rich and give to the poor. I mention this not to make a political statement or pass any kind of moral judgment on any particular company. However, the reality is that certain companies, due to the nature of the business, are more of a target for hacker activism. It is also important to realize that an event that gets a lot of bad press, either specific to your company or to the industry you're in, could make for a temporary increase in hacker attacks against your network.

World events also make companies in a given country more of a target for international hackers. On September 11, 2001, there was a huge increase in computer-related attacks from international hackers against companies in the United States. This type of electronic warfare is very disconcerting for several reasons. For one thing, a nation's foreign policies can have a real effect on how other countries perceive them. Both Great Britain and the United States have taken broad actions to combat terrorism. Such actions will always garner strong supporters as well as strong opponents. Hackers will try to attack companies in particular countries for such political reasons. If your company has overseas facilities, they may be targets as well. Hackers may attack overseas facilities because they don't like the fact that a "foreign power" is conducting business in their country. It also gives them a way to attack you without having to leave their own country.

Another issue with international hackers is that they can often act with almost total impunity. Depending on the international relations, the "host" country may even covertly support what they are doing. The country in which the hacker resides may not have laws that make such activities illegal. Even if they are illegal in the particular country, what are the costs involved for your company to press criminal charges against a hacker who lives halfway around the world? How serious would a particular hacking event have to be for your company to try and press changes against an individual that lived in countries such as Russia, India, or China?

Aside from the difficulties in attempting to press criminal charges, you're not going to sue a hacker living in any of those countries either. Even if such a civil suit were possible, the legal costs would be prohibitive. The average hacker in a Third World country would almost certainly lack the financial resources to go after anyway. Your strongest protection against becoming a victim of such an event is to put up the best defenses you possibly can.

SCRIPT KIDDIES

Another troubling trend is that, as computers and software programs become more sophisticated, it's easier to be a hacker. Anybody can download a whole host of hacking tools from the Internet. Most of these programs are both free and relatively easy to use. They don't require a low-skilled hacker to write any kind of program; everything is scripted out for them in the application itself. Most have a graphical user interface (GUI), making them even easier to use. This has led to the phenomenon of what I call the casual hacker or "script kiddie." These people generally don't possess in-depth computer programming knowledge. They are computer savvy enough to know how to surf the Internet and how to use computer hacking tools. In this day and age, many young people start using computers in the first grade. So, by the time they're teenagers, they have ten years' computer experience. For a script kiddie, that's more than enough expertise to cause trouble. In most Western countries, access to computers is quite prevalent. A very high percentage of households in the United States have one or more computers in them. These hacking tools are very effective against computers that are not properly patched or that are not protected by current anti-virus software. While many believe that such unprotected systems are more often found in the home, that's really not the case. A lack of up-to-date patching and current anti-virus software is just as prevalent in the business environment as it is on home computers. This presents a greater risk in a business setting since corporations are more of a target for hackers than home systems are.

FRAUDSTERS

Consider the leap of faith that we all take when we hand our credit cards over to complete strangers at the end of a meal at a restaurant. Unlike most other transactions, waiters and waitresses take our cards, and then leave for several minutes to complete the transaction. Just how hard would it be for them to write down the name, account number, expiration date, and any security code the card may have on it? In most cases, that's all the information that is needed to make purchases with the credit card either online or over the phone. People can steal our credit card information when we are standing right in front of them. When we hand our credit cards over to a cashier, we often have to sign either a paper receipt or on a signature pad to complete the transaction. This will divert our attention, if only for a few moments.

There's a device available over the Internet that's called a skimming wedge. It's very small, easily fitting in the palm of your hand. A skimming wedge is basically a tiny card reader. The cashier/fraudster can have it hidden behind the counter, and swipe the credit cards of unsuspecting customers when they are signing for their legitimate transactions. The skimming wedge will capture all of the information that is encoded on the back of a credit card. That's all it takes: a couple of seconds and the fraudster has all the information they need to use our credit cards.

PROSECUTING HACKERS

A common thread among hackers is that in most cases they don't get prosecuted. That could be due to the country the hacker resides in, or the difficulty in determining "beyond a reasonable doubt" the precise individual who performed a particular electronic attack. As mentioned, some countries quietly support cyber attacks against the West. If hackers are actually on the payroll of a foreign government, the odds of them facing any criminal prosecution is zero. In cases like this, the hacker may actually be considered to be engaging in electronic warfare. Either way, the results are the same; your network is under attack.

Some countries simply will not extradite their citizens for allegedly committing a cyber crime. Consider the fact that Russia will not grant Britain's motion for the extradition of Andrei Lugovoi, who is suspected of murdering Alexander Litvinenko, a former KGB agent. Mr. Litvinenko suffered a particularly painful death after being poisoned by a radioactive substance. The charge is that Andrei Lugovoi placed the poison in Mr. Litvinenko's tea. If the Russian authorities are unwilling to extradite one of their citizens on a charge of murder, hackers have very little to be concerned about.

Consider the odds of somebody being extradited from a Middle Eastern country for hacking a company that is located in either the United States or Great Britain. For that matter, would Hugo Chavez of Venezuela be quick to punish one of his citizens for hacking a United States government Web site? This is the same man who stood up at the United Nations and called President George W. Bush "Satan." The reality is that in many countries, successful hacking activities would likely brand you a patriot or a hero, and not a criminal.

Another phenomenon that makes it difficult to prosecute hackers is the difficulty in assigning a dollar value to certain types of computer crime. What is the cost if a hacker causes a temporary system outage or a slowdown? If a particular system has appropriate backup, perhaps very little. Yet, if somebody were to throw a brick through an office window, the damage is much more tangible. They wouldn't use the fact that the building had several other windows as a defense. Computer hackers know that even if they are discovered, the odds of them facing any criminal prosecution are very slight.

In fact, one of the biggest challenges for security professionals is convincing companies to spend money for security. The same phenomenon that makes it difficult to assign to dollar value to some of the damage caused by hackers makes it difficult to justify spending money on security.

As is true with most very technical issues, it is best to explain the intricacies in non-technical terms. Here is a scenario I outlined for a group of executives who worked for various large financial institutions. I told the group that I had just found a way to save them million of dollars. I would replace all the heavy metal vault doors with hollow-core wood doors painted to look like they were made out of metal. Since wood is much cheaper, they would realize a huge cost savings. They could also sell the metal doors and make even more money. The absurdity of the suggestion was very obvious to everyone. I went on to argue that a hollow-core wooden door only puts individual vaults at risk. On the other hand, poor information security measures can put an entire network's data resources at risk.

The point is simple. If you need to persuade executives to loosen the purse strings for security, phrase your arguments in terms that are easily understandable to your target audience.

ANTI-VIRUS AND PATCHING SOFTWARE

If you're involved in purchasing security software for your company, then you already know that beyond the initial costs of the anti-virus software, there's the fee to receive regular updates as they become available. The bad guys are always writing new viruses to try and infect computer systems. This requires anti-virus companies to write appropriate inoculants to protect computers from the new viruses. Another disturbing trend is that the amount of time from when a new virus is written to when it may infect your systems is changing. What was once measured in days or hours in the past has now been reduced to minutes. This puts pressure on companies that write anti-virus software to be prepared to write a program to combat the latest virus very quickly. It also puts pressure on companies to install updated anti-virus files just as quickly. The ability to fully test new anti-virus files to make sure there aren't any compatibility issues with any of your company's computer is strained. You are left with the risk of not fully testing the latest anti-virus file, or being exposed to the latest virus.

The good news is that there are things you can do, besides quickly installing the latest anti-virus file, to protect your systems from viruses. Many software manufacturers will issue software fixes to address vulnerabilities found in their applications after their initial release. Such after-the-fact software fixes are often referred to as patches. Ensuring that your systems are fully patched as appropriate will help strengthen their immunity against viruses. I'm speaking in quasi-human terms to illustrate a point. Just as healthy people who eat right, exercise, and take their vitamins are better able to fight off a cold or the flu, a "healthy" computer is also more resistant electronic viruses. Whenever a patch is offered, then, be sure to install it quickly.

VIRUSES—TROJANS—WORMS

Viruses, Trojans, worms, and other forms of malware (purposely harmful software) can cause havoc on a company's computer network. Code Red,

Nimda, and other highly publicized forms of malicious software have done a lot of damage in their day. Companies can take a variety of counter-measures to combat the effects of malware. As mentioned above, anti-virus software is a must-have. Keep it current, and keep it running. Acknowledging that certain Internet sites are more apt to contain viruses, I recommend that companies have a policy to block such sites. The administrative control of a policy should be combined with technical controls.

It is technically possible to block, or severely limit, the Internet sites that your employees can visit from their work computers. Websense is an example of software that can be loaded onto end-user systems to block access to Web sites deemed inappropriate. Since it's loaded directly on the end-users' systems, it can enforce Internet usage policies even when the system is not attached to the company's network. This is important for laptops users who may connect to the Internet without connecting to their company's network in an effort to visit prohibited web sites. Most Web browsing software such as Microsoft's Internet Explorer allow users to filter out Web sites based on objectionable content. Web sites with strong adult content, in addition to being deemed offensive, particularly in a business setting, are generally not the best at policing themselves to ensure they are free of viruses. In essence, a Web site may be dirty on several levels.

When users try to connect to the Internet from within a company's network, the sites that they are allowed to visit can be controlled by any number of technical controls. Web sites have IP addresses, which can be blocked by a company's perimeter firewalls. Companies can also monitor the Web sites that their employees are visiting, and approach them if repeated visits to unapproved sites become an issue.

SPYWARE, ADWARE, AND TRACKING COOKIES

There are other types of software that, while not necessarily malicious in nature, can cause privacy concerns. Spyware will take personal information from your computer without either your knowledge or consent. It can be relatively benign, merely tracking which Internet sites you visit, or much more malicious in nature. On a more fraudulent level, spyware can also log your keystrokes to steal usernames and passwords, and even record any information contained on your computer's hard drive.

Adware is a different problem. If you see ads for various companies and products pop up on your computer seemingly out of nowhere, you have what is known as adware on your system. Companies will bundle ads with their "free" software as a way to defer costs. In many instances, once you pay for a copy of the software, the ads will stop popping up. Google and other software providers have products that will block most pop-up ads.

Companies that sell products over the Internet will send what's called a "cookie" to your computer. The cookie allows them to keep track of your computer, and the fact that you've visited their Web site. While spyware, adware, and cookies are not as damaging as viruses, they can cause problems. Over time, a sufficient number of these types of programs can accumulate on a computer and cause performance issues. From a privacy standpoint, it is best to try to block these types of programs as well. Web browsing software such as Microsoft's Internet Explorer can be set to block cookies. There are also companies that sell software that will scan your computer and attempt to remove these types of programs. Spybot is a well known program that does just that, and it is available for free over the Internet.

BLACK LIST—WHITE LIST

The ever-increasing challenge is to try and keep up with all of the new viruses that are constantly being written. Anti-virus software is a reactive type of technology, because it works off of known virus signatures. The challenge then becomes racing to update your company's anti-virus software to be able to recognize the latest virus, sometime known as a zero-hour virus. A known list of "bad" software is also called a "black list."

Companies such as Verdasys have developed products that take a different approach. Rather than maintaining a list of known bad software, they maintain a list of known good software, or a "white list."

With a white list approach, a company would note what software is allowed to run on their network and systems and take a pre-determined action upon detecting unrecognized software. The unknown software could be blocked outright, or could trigger an alert to a system administrator to determine the appropriate course of action. Such a "deny that which is not expressly allowed" approach effectively blocks even unknown viruses. While I would not recommend that a company get rid of their anti-virus software, incorporating a white list-type product into a company's network would be a strong defense-in-depth strategy.

COMPLEXITY OF SYSTEMS—EASE OF ATTACK

As computer systems and networks have become more advanced, not only have they made life easier for legitimate purposes, but they have also aided the hacker and the virus programmer. Prior to the Internet it was impossible for a computer virus to spread across systems in different companies located around the world. Today, a virus can spread around the world very quickly. You don't even need to be physically connected to a network—you can introduce the latest virus over the airways by using wireless technology.

Computers of the past, the 1980s to early 1990s, were very limited in both capacity and function compared to what we have today. The fact that older computers were limited in so many ways actually made them harder to infect with a virus. They didn't contain millions or even billions of lines of software code now required to run their applications. Such a vast code base contains any number of vulnerabilities a virus can take advantage of.

A support engineer had a lot less to contend with on systems that ran MS-DOS as its operating system and had a hard-drive capacity of 10 megabytes or less. With today's computers being capable of performing far more work, with hard drive space measured in gigabytes and terabytes, it's much easier to find areas to exploit. I've mentioned the need to properly configure servers so they only do the work they are intended to do. As they become more complex, that task becomes both more important and more difficult.

The most secure computer is one that is doing exactly what you expect and nothing else. That was much easier to accomplish on older systems. However, you can make the task of securing computers easier by implementing the following procedure: dedicate computer systems to performing as few functions as possible. For example, use a Web server only as a Web server. Don't store sensitive data on the same computer; use a separate database or application server for that. You make the work of the would-be hacker much easier if the data they are trying to steal is stored on an Internet-facing Web server. They only have to hack the one server, and they don't have to contend with any firewalls, intrusion detection sensors, or a separate physical server.

Using this type of electronic "separation of duties" has benefits for availability as well. Consider the impact if you had a problem with a single system that functioned as a Web sever, a database server, an e-mail server, and an application server. A glitch in any one of the functions would affect the server as a whole and all the functions just mentioned. Something as benign as having to reboot the system as part of applying the latest security patch would impact everything.

I therefore strongly recommend having dedicated e-mail servers, dedicated database servers, dedicated application servers, and so forth. Due to the complexity of today's applications, most database engineers are not the best individuals to support e-mails servers, and vice versa. Asking somebody to support a single system performing multiple functions in this manner can cause problems; it's better to have specialists in each area if budget permits.

SECURITY OF SENSITIVE DATA ON PAPER

While most companies have a certain level of awareness that they need to protect data in electronic form, many forget the need to protect data that is on good old-fashioned paper. Dumpster divers, cleaning crews, and visitors with cell phone cameras can all exploit poor controls around sensitive data on paper. So, have a clean-desk policy that discourages employees from leaving sensitive data lying around in plain sight. Obviously, employees may need to have sensitive documents on their desks while working, but they should protect them when they leave for lunch, a break, or even just to go to the restroom. When they leave for the night, employees should be required to place sensitive documents in a locked cabinet.

The secure disposal of documents is another part of a comprehensive defense-in-depth protection of your company's sensitive data. Some companies opt to have shredders on-site, requiring employees to destroy sensitive documents themselves. There are companies that provide secure document disposal. Two that I am aware of are Recall and Iron Mountain. Document disposal companies will provide you with secure trash bins. They are basically large garbage cans with lockable lids on them. The lids have a slit on them wide enough to place documents into the containers, but too small for anybody to reach in and remove any papers. But watch out—during on-site inspections, I have actually found secure bins with no padlock on the lids. Without the padlock securing the lid, the secure disposal container becomes a trash can with a lid on it. Ensure that the lid is secured with a locked padlock. Place tight controls around who has either the combination or the key to unlock the padlock. In situations where a company is going to place a lot of paper into secure bins, you may want to open them to allow for quicker disposal. However, these cases should be rare and closely monitored. The bins should be locked again as soon as possible.

Some disposal companies will shred on-site, bringing huge shredders right to your facility to destroy all the documents prior to taking them off-site. That is, of course, the most secure way to ensure that your company's sensitive data has been properly disposed of. In addition to secure disposal and a clean-desk policy, take care as to what data you have in unsecured files on your desk, or what is pinned up on the walls of your cube or office.

Leaving the decision up to your entire employee base to determine what data on paper is sensitive enough to be shredded is a risk in and of itself. There's also the potential for laziness, as the trash can that is right by their feet is much more convenient then having to go to the secure disposal bin to throw our paper trash away. Some companies have implemented what could be referred to as a wet-dry trash policy. Wet trash, such as sandwich bags, banana peels, apple cores, and the like can be thrown away in unprotected garbage cans. Dry trash (paper) can only be disposed of in secure document disposal bins. This removes any discretion on the part of the employee as to whether the data on a particular piece of paper is sensitive or not.

Such a policy will reduce the odds of sensitive data being improperly disposed of. It will also make it easier for managers, information security officers, and compliance officers to ensure the policy is being followed. With a wet-dry trash policy, you only need to see if there is any paper at all in a regular office garbage to see if procedures are being followed. That is much easier, and less intrusive, then having to actually remove a piece of paper trash from a garbage can to determine if it contains sensitive data or not. It's not enough for dumpster divers merely to steal sensitive data on paper that was not disposed of properly; in some cases they publicize the event on the Internet. In May 2007, a video on YouTube, a popular Internet site, showed sensitive customer data that dumpster divers have found on customers of Chase bank. Obviously an embarrassing situation for Chase to have to deal with.

CDS AND OTHER STORAGE DEVICES

Sensitive data on other physical mediums such as CDs and backup tapes needs to be protected also. While it is not possible to encrypt sensitive data on paper, it is possible to encrypt data on these types of removable electronic storage devices. The same policies that pertain to encrypting sensitive data while on a computer should apply when the data is on removable media. When such media are to be destroyed, ensure that they are totally destroyed. Industrial-strength shredders can handle CDs. There are companies that will shred backup tapes and hard drives. Bear in mind that a hacker could retrieve data from length of tape as short as only a couple of inches long. You may also want to consider burning backup tapes as part of the disposal process.

MAILING SENSITIVE DATA

Due care needs to be taken to protect sensitive data when being sent through the mail, whether you're using a private mail carrier such as DHL, FedEx, or UPS, or your government's public mail system. When mailing sensitive data on electronic media, ensure that the data is encrypted. Even though you can't encrypt data that is on paper, you can employ measures to protect the information. Most mail carriers provide services that require the intended recipient to sign for the package upon receipt. Larger mail carriers also provide for electronic tracking of packages for an additional fee. Such precautions are advisable when sending any kind of sensitive materials through the mail. Do not label the outside of the package in a way that will advise everybody of the nature of the contents. This can have the effect of making the package more of a target for data thieves.

Suffice it to say, the bad guys (hackers) are out there, and they are getting more resourceful all the time. It's why the field of data security is an ever-changing discipline that needs to adapt to new challenges as well as to changes in technology. It's also why it is important to hire the best and brightest security professionals in the field to help protect your company's electronic assets. Once you've hired them, it's important that they keep their skills current by attending regular training sessions.

CHAPTER 8

PERSONNEL ISSUES AND HIRING PRACTICES

Your staff, of course, has a great impact on the security of all your operations. There are numerous things to consider when it comes to personnel issues and hiring practices. These include effective recruiting, performing background checks, conducting drug screening, and making certain new hires agree to your company's policies. Then, once you have a great team in place, you have to retain them. Just as building a secure network is far less expensive than making a network secure, retention is much cheaper than recruitment. And retention is also a security issue—when you have high turnover, you are bound to have disgruntled employees who may steal data or physical items, or sabotage your operations.

It is also important to hire the best when it comes to hiring information security personnel. The protection of electronic data is such a new discipline that many companies are struggling with finding the qualified people. It's not that they are not out there. But unless you're an active practitioner, it can be problematic at best to try and recognize the talent during the recruitment process. This is not to say that non-security managers and human resources professionals shouldn't be involved in the recruitment process. However, somewhere within the recruitment process, it is best that security candidates be interviewed by professionals with a strong security background themselves.

Many companies are rushing to implement risk-assessment tools in an effort to interject a certain amount of automation into the risk-assessment process. While such tools can certainly help, all of the risk-assessment tools and comprehensive security policies cannot replace highly skilled professionals with extensive backgrounds in technology and security. It would be akin to relying on WebMD to make all of your medical decisions, and never consulting a doctor.

In this chapter, we'll discuss a few things related to all the people you bring on board. Then we'll discuss the ins and outs of hiring information security personnel. But let's start this chapter by talking about who not to hire.

THE JANITOR WITH A PH.D.

Watch out for people with advanced computer backgrounds that apply for unusually low-level jobs. For example, don't hire an applicant with a Ph.D. in computer science to be part of your company's night janitorial crew. This person is a hacker. It is a common hacker trick to seek out low-level jobs that grant them access to your company. This points to the importance of performing background checks for positions that may be deemed non-sensitive, perhaps not at the same level as with more critical positions, but a certain amount of due diligence is appropriate. The truth is that companies will perform only cursory background checks, if any at all, for such non-sensitive positions. The hackers know this all too well. Since most companies contract with third parties to provide both janitorial and uniformed security services, the hacker can get access to your company without ever going through your normal screening processes. As a result, you may want to re-evaluate your hiring practices for both your janitorial as well as you uniformed security guard staff.

Both janitors and night security guards generally have access to most, if not all, of the areas within a given facility, and usually with little scrutiny. People don't generally micro-manage somebody to ensure that the trash cans are being emptied properly. Both janitors and night-shift security personnel generally work at a time when buildings are either empty or have only a skeleton crew. Since a janitor needs access to all parts of a building to empty the trash, they'll likely have access to all the executives' offices, as well as all the normally restricted computer areas.

How much sensitive data is left out on desks and tacked up to walls in your company? The hacker/janitor doesn't even have to physically take the documents in order to steal the information. A cell phone equipped with a camera will allow them to steal all the data that is left in plain site, without anybody being the wiser. As thoughts of a clean-desk policy are going through your mind right now, don't forget the issue of white boards. They are great for brain storming and strategic planning in meetings. Does your company ever have instances where people write "do not erase" on the white board? That only identifies the information as sensitive. Your company's Ph.D. janitor could be looking to steal such information for identity theft, or be one of your competitors involved in industrial espionage.

Security guards are perhaps more of a risk then janitors. Security guards are generally given computer access so that they can perform tasks such as issuing ID badges, observing and tracking access alerts, and monitoring the activity captured by a company's closed-circuit camera system. A security guard working away at a computer terminal is nothing that would generally arouse anybody's suspicion. You could literally be giving a hacker his very own user account and a computer terminal in which to steal your company's sensitive information.

Strict limitations should be placed on any type of system access given to uniformed security personnel. Ideally, the systems they need to access to perform their functions should be totally separate from other systems in your network that contain sensitive information. For example, security guards often have access to a list of company personnel to assist visitors. Generally, the necessary information should be limited to a person's name, phone number, and where they work in the building. You should provide a separate list that provides only the required information. Do not provide them access to the same system that also contains things like Social Security numbers, salary information, health records, disciplinary actions, etc. If your company utilizes security controls to monitor the activity of users with access to sensitive computer data, include the computer terminals utilized by security guards in your deployment strategy.

BACKGROUND CHECKS

Depending on the nature of the business that your company is in, you may be required by any number of governmental regulations to perform background checks on prospective new hires. I believe it's a good idea to perform background checks for all new hires. It's not only important to protect your company's data, but it's even more important to protect your employees as well. You'd want to know if a prospective new hire has a history of violent criminal activity.

I am greatly disturbed, for example, when I hear that somebody with a criminal record in another state for being a sex offender has managed to get hired in a local school. While I may be getting off the topic of data security, nothing is more important than protecting our children. In certain sensitive positions, especially for those that involve working with children, nationwide background checks would be best.

Criminal history background checks that go back seven or more years are relatively common. State-level checks are better than only checking the local municipality. This would include checking every state that the applicant has lived in during the past seven years. Now, a seven year background check will only work if somebody has lived in the United States for the past seven years. This issue comes into play for temporary foreign workers who may have lived in the United States for only a short period of time. If the prospective employee has only been in the country for the past six months, that limits your U.S.-based background check.

If I'm a "bad guy," I just need to keep my nose clean for the short time I'm in the country to successfully pass any domestic criminal history background check.

Depending on what country your company is located in and the nature of the business you're in, you will be regulated by any number of laws mandating that you know who you are hiring. If your company has a multinational presence, the applicant screening requirements will vary from country to country. In the United States, for example, you'll need to verify employment eligibility on the I-9 form.

There are certain crimes that constitute what is sometimes referred to as a breach of trust. Some examples would include: accepting a bribe, insider trading, falsification of official documentation (such as a company's financial statement), and more. Individuals convicted of these types of criminal acts are generally banned from ever holding a wide range of sensitive positions.

Banks, pharmaceutical companies, and businesses and government agencies that deal with highly sensitive information, therefore, need to ensure that their applicants are not in such bad financial shape themselves as to present a risk if placed in a sensitive position. In these instances, a financial background check is needed in addition to a criminal history check. The reasoning here is that such persons are deemed to be more easily bribed, or to be recruited by foreign governments to pass on classified information. People in financial difficulty are more apt to defraud a bank or to steal medicines from a pharmacy or hospital.

And then there are the known bad guys you need to keep out. Table 8.1 below provides a list of agencies and watch lists from several counties around the world. Depending on where your company is located and the specific nature of your business, you may be required by law to check against any number of them prior to extending a job offer to any candidate. A candidate may be ineligible for employment based on what country they are from, and the particular relations between that country and the government where your company is located.

EQUAL EMPLOYMENT OPPORTUNITY COMMISSION

All hiring managers need to understand some of the laws regarding the entire employment process from recruiting to separation.

For example, in the United States, the Equal Employment Opportunity Commission (EEOC) requires that hiring decisions not be based on issues such as an applicant's age, gender, race, or religion. The EEOC's mandate is specified under Title VII of the Civil Rights Act of 1964, the Equal Pay Act, the Age Discrimination in Employment Act (ADEA), the Rehabilitation Act of 1973, and the Americans with Disabilities Act (ADA).

Table 8.1: Watch Lists

Agency	Web site
United States	
OFAC Specially Designated Nationals & Blocked Persons	http://www.treas.gov/offices/eotffc/ofac/index.html
OFAC Sanctioned Countries	http://www.ustreas.gov/offices/eotffc/ofac/sanctions/
Department of State Trade Control Debarred Parties	http://www.pmdtc.org/debar059.htm
U.S. Bureau of Industry & Security (formerly BXA) Unverified Entities List Denied Entities List Denied Persons List	http://www.bxa.doc.gov/Enforcement/Unverifiedlist/unverified_parties.html http://www.bxa.doc.gov/Entities/Default.htm http://www.bis.doc.gov/dpl/Default.shtm
FBI Most Wanted Terrorists & Seeking Information	http://www.fbi.gov/mostwant//terrorists/fugitives.htm http://www.fbi.gov/terrorinfo/terrorismsi.htm
FBI Top Ten Most Wanted	http://www.fbi.gov/mostwant//topten/fugitives/fugitives.htm
England and Canada	
Bank of England Sanctions List	http://www.bankofengland.co.uk/publications/financialsanctions/faqs/faqs_consolidated_list.htm
OSFI - Canadian Sanctions List	http://www.osfi-bsif.gc.ca/osfi/index_e.aspx?DetailID=525
Lists maintained by International Organizations	
INTERPOL Most Wanted List	http://www.interpol.int/Public/Wanted/Search/Recent.asp
Politically Exposed Persons List	http://www.complinet.com/kyccheck/kyccheck/pep.html
World Bank Ineligible Firms	http://web.worldbank.org/
Non-Cooperative Countries and Territories	http://www1.oecd.org/fatf/NCCT_en.htm
European Union Terrorism List	http://www.statewatch.org/news/2004/jun/01terrlists.htm
United Nations Consolidated Sanctions List	http://www.un.org/docs/sc/committees/1267/tablelist.htm

Under these laws and other federal, state, and local laws, it is illegal to discriminate in any aspect of employment, including:

- Hiring and firing;
- Compensation, assignment, or classification of employees;
- Transfer, promotion, layoff, or recall;
- Job advertisements;
- Recruitment;
- Testing;
- Use of company facilities;
- Training and apprenticeship programs;
- Fringe benefits;
- Pay, retirement plans, and disability leave; or
- Other terms and conditions of employment.

Discriminatory practices under these laws also include:

- Harassment on the basis of race, color, religion, sex, national origin, disability, or age;
- Retaliation against an individual for filing a charge of discrimination, participating in an investigation, or opposing discriminatory practices;
- Employment decisions based on stereotypes or assumptions about the abilities, traits, or performance of individuals of a certain sex, race, age, religion, or ethnic group, or individuals with disabilities; and
- Denying employment opportunities to a person because of marriage to, or association with, an individual of a particular race, religion, national origin, or an individual with a disability. Title VII also prohibits discrimination because of participation in schools or places of worship associated with a particular racial, ethnic, or religious group.

Employers are required to post notices to all employees advising them of their rights under the laws EEOC enforces and their right to be free from retaliation. Such notices must be accessible, as needed, to persons with visual or other disabilities that affect reading.

Title VII prohibits not only intentional discrimination, but also practices that have the effect of discriminating against individuals because of their race, color, national origin, religion, or sex. Specific to national origin, the EEOC states:

- It is illegal to discriminate against an individual because of birthplace, ancestry, culture, or linguistic characteristics common to a specific ethnic group.
- A rule requiring that employees speak only English on the job may violate Title VII unless an employer shows that the requirement is necessary for conducting

business. If the employer believes such a rule is necessary, employees must be informed when English is required and the consequences for violating the rule.

On the one hand, the Immigration Reform and Control Act (IRCA) of 1986 requires employers to ensure that employees hired are legally authorized to work in the United States. However, an employer who requests employment verification only for individuals of a particular national origin, or individuals who appear to be or sound foreign, may violate both Title VII and IRCA; verification must be obtained from all applicants and employees. Employers who impose citizenship requirements or give preferences to U.S. citizens in hiring or employment opportunities also may violate IRCA.

Specific to religious accommodation, the laws the EEOC enforces require that an employer reasonably accommodate the religious belief of an employee or prospective employee, unless doing so would impose an undue hardship.

With regards to sexual discrimination, Title VII's broad prohibitions specifically cover:

- Sexual Harassment. This includes practices ranging from direct requests for sexual favors to workplace conditions that create a hostile environment for persons of either gender, including same-sex harassment. (The "hostile environment" standard also applies to harassment on the basis of race, color, national origin, religion, age, and disability.)
- Pregnancy-Based Discrimination. Pregnancy, childbirth, and related medical conditions must be treated in the same way as other temporary illnesses or conditions. (This is actually part of the 1978 Pregnancy Discrimination Act, which is an amendment to Title VII of the 1964 Civil Rights Act.)

The law also prohibits age discrimination, specifically:

- Statements or specifications in job notices or advertisements of age preference and limitations. An age limit may only be specified in the rare circumstance where age has been proven to be a *bona fide* occupational qualification (BFOQ);
- Discrimination on the basis of age by apprenticeship programs, including joint labor-management apprenticeship programs; and
- Denial of benefits to older employees. An employer may reduce benefits based on age only if the cost of providing the reduced benefits to older workers is the same as the cost of providing benefits to younger workers.

The Equal Pay Act (EPA) prohibits discrimination on the basis of sex in the payment of wages or benefits, where men and women perform work of similar skill, effort, and responsibility for the same employer under similar working conditions. The EPA goes on to note that:

- Employers may not reduce wages of either sex to equalize pay between men and women.
- A violation of the EPA may occur where a different wage was/is paid to a person who worked in the same job before or after an employee of the opposite sex.
- A violation may also occur where a labor union causes the employer to violate the law.

THE AMERICANS WITH DISABILITIES ACT

The Americans with Disabilities Act (ADA) prohibits discrimination on the basis of disability in all employment practices. It is necessary to understand several important ADA definitions to know who is protected by the law and what constitutes illegal discrimination.

Individual with a Disability

An individual with a disability under the ADA is defined as a person who has either a physical or a mental impairment that substantially limits one or more major life activities, has a record of such an impairment, or is regarded as having such an impairment. Major life activities are activities that an average person can perform with little or no difficulty, such as walking, breathing, seeing, hearing, speaking, learning, and working.

Qualified Individual with a Disability

As defined by the ADA, a qualified employee or applicant with a disability is someone who satisfies skill, experience, education, and other job-related requirements of the position held or desired, and who, with or without reasonable accommodation, can perform the essential functions of that position.

Reasonable Accommodation

The ADA states that reasonable accommodation may include, but is not limited to, making existing facilities used by employees readily accessible to and usable by persons with disabilities; job restructuring; modification of work schedules; providing additional unpaid leave; reassignment to a vacant position; acquiring or modifying equipment or devices; adjusting or modifying examinations, training materials, or policies; and providing qualified readers or interpreters. Reasonable accommodation may be necessary to apply for a job, to perform job functions, or to enjoy the benefits and privileges of employment enjoyed by people without disabilities. An employer is not required to lower production standards to make an accommodation. An employer generally is not obligated to provide personal use items such as eyeglasses or hearing aids.

Undue Hardship

An employer is required to make a reasonable accommodation to a qualified individual with a disability unless they can demonstrate that doing so would impose an undue hardship on the operation of the employer's business. Undue hardship is defined as an action that requires significant difficulty or cost when considered in relation to factors such as a business's size, financial resources, and the nature and structure of its operation.

Prohibited Inquiries and Examinations

Before making an offer of employment, an employer is forbidden from asking a job applicant about the existence, nature, or severity of a disability. Applicants may be asked about their ability to perform job functions. A job offer may be conditioned on the results of a medical examination, but only if the examination is required for all persons entering in the same job category. Medical examinations of employees must also be job-related and consistent with business necessity.

Drug and Alcohol Use

Employees and applicants currently engaging in the illegal use of drugs are not protected by the ADA when an employer acts on the basis of such use. Testing for evidence of illegal drug use is not considered a medical examination and, therefore, is not subject to the ADA's restrictions on medical examinations. Employers may hold individuals who are illegally using drugs and individuals with alcoholism to the same standards of performance as other employees.

DRUG SCREENING

As noted above, conducting drug and alcohol screenings is not prohibited by federal employment laws. The government recognizes the inherent risks that people under the influence of such substances pose in the workplace. It becomes even more critical if your company is in some sort of manufacturing business that deals with heavy machinery, or utilizes professional drivers, especially if your company transports hazardous material, and of course any pharmaceutical-related industry. As a parent, I would want to be very certain that bus drivers, teachers, counselors, and any other employees working in the schools are subject to both background checks and drug screenings.

Again, conducting drug screening is a security issue in another sense—people doing drugs need money to buy them, and they may think it's OK to steal from their employers to pay for their habit.

HIRING TECH WORKERS: RECRUITING AND INDUSTRY CERTIFICATIONS

It's hard enough hiring good people for any position in the company. It's especially hard to find good technical employees. A challenge that many companies face when trying to bring on qualified applicants is where best to spend their advertising dollars. There are a slew of sites on the Internet that advertise jobs for technical, security, and auditor-related positions. These include: Dice, Monster, IT CareerNet, ITclassified, ITjobs, and many more. Many will allow employers to post their job openings, which in turn allows applicants to see who is hiring. Many of these sites will also allow applicants to post their resumes, enabling recruiters to search for potential applicants online. A word of caution here: these sites do not perform any kind of checks to ensure an applicant posting a resume actually has the skills and background that they claim to have. You must exercise the usual due diligence.

However, there are member-only sites that require that you hold a recognized certification before you can upload your resume. The International Information Systems Security Certification Consortium, Inc., ISC^2, is an international security consortium that among other things issues security-related certifications, including the CISSP, Certified Information System Security Professional. Individuals who have their resumes posted on their site, www.isc2.org, will possess at least a CISSP certification and in most cases several others as well. There are other well-respected security industry certifications as well, such as the Global Information Assurance Certification (GIAC) from the System Administration, Networking, and Security Institute (SANS).

You should perform other forms of due diligence to get an accurate assessment of an applicant's qualifications. If you're hiring an information security professional, asking technical questions, security questions, as well as questions about specific government regulations such as CA S.B. 1386 are all fair game. I also consider anything that an applicant puts on their resume specific to their education and professional experience to be fair territory for inquiry. For example, if you say that you have five years of experience working as a firewall engineer, I expect you to know something about them.

Industry-recognized certifications give an applicant a certain degree of credibility, while at the same time offer some level of assurance to companies of their backgrounds. The following tables provide a list of both technical as well as security related certifications. The certifications listed in Tables 8.2, 8.3, and 8.4 are by no means a comprehensive list of every industry certification world wide, but the are some of the better known. While such certifications are not a guarantee that your new hire will be a resounding success, they show a certain level of experience and maturity in the field.

The Information Systems Audit and Control Association (ISACA) has both the CISA and the CISM. The Certified Information Systems Auditor (CISA) certification is the globally accepted standard of achievement among information systems audit, control, and security professionals. The Certified Information Security Manager (CISM) certification program is developed specifically for experienced information security managers and those who have information security management responsibilities.

There are some emerging yet promising certifications, such as the Holistic Information Security Practitioner (HISP) Certification. It is promoted by the British Standards Institute (BSI), which provides practical education on the integration of best practices for Information Security Management, Information Systems Auditing, and multiple regulatory compliance requirements.

There are also certifications for the various versions of Linux. For example, Red Hat has the Red Hat Certified Technician (RHCT) and Red Hat Certified Engineer (RHCE). RHCT is the first step in establishing Linux credentials and is an ideal certification for those transitioning from non-UNIX/Linux environments. RHCE, called the "crown jewel of Linux certifications," proves an individual's ability to configure networking services and security on servers running a Red Hat operating system.

IN SEARCH OF THE ALL KNOWING

It's important to know what you want in an employee, and to have realistic expectations for a new hire's qualifications. Putting unrealistic expectations in the job description indicates that, as an employer,

Table 8.2: Cisco Certifications

Certification Path	Associate	Professional	Expert
Routing & Switching	CCNA	CCNP	CCIE Routing & Switching
Design	CCNA & CCDA	CCDP	None
Network Security	CCNA	CCSP	CCIE Security
Service Provider	CCNA	CCIP	CCIE Service Provider
Storage Networking	CCNA	None	CCIE Storage Networking
Voice	CCAN	CCVP	CCIE Voice

Table 8.3: Microsoft Certifications

MCTS	Microsoft Certified Technology Specialist	Enables professionals to target specific technologies and to distinguish themselves by demonstrating in-depth knowledge and expertise in the various Microsoft specialized technologies.
MCITP	Microsoft Certified IT Professional	Demonstrates comprehensive skills in planning, deploying, supporting, maintaining, and optimizing IT infrastructures.
MCPD	Microsoft Certified Professional Developer	Distinguish an individual as an expert Windows Application Developer, Web Application Developer, or Enterprise Applications Developer, using .Net.
MCAD	Microsoft Certified Application Developer	An individual is certified to use Microsoft technologies to develop and maintain department-level applications, components, Web or desktop clients, or back-end data services.
MCDST	Microsoft Certified Desktop Support Technician	Certifies that an individual has the technical skills to troubleshoot hardware and software operation issues in Microsoft Windows environments.
MCT	Microsoft Certified Trainer	Individuals who are qualified instructors to deliver Microsoft training courses to IT professionals and developers.
MCLC	Microsoft Certified Learning Consultant	This credential recognizes MCTs whose job roles have grown to include frequent consultative engagements with customers. These MCTs are experts in designing and delivering customized learning solutions.
MCSE	Microsoft Certified Systems Engineer	An individual is certified to design and implement an infrastructure solution that is based on the Windows operating system and Microsoft Windows Server System software. Specializations include MCSE: Messaging and MCSE: Security.
MCSA	Microsoft Certified Systems Administrators	An individual is certified to administer network and systems environments based on the Microsoft Windows operating systems. Specializations include MCSA: Messaging and MCSA: Security.

MCDBA	Microsoft Certified Database Administrator	An individual is certified to design, implement and administer Microsoft SQL server databases.
MCSD	Microsoft Certified Solution Developers	An individual is certified to design and develop leading-edge business solutions with Microsoft development tools, technologies, platforms, and the Microsoft Windows architecture.

you don't have a strong sense of what kind of employee that you are looking for. I see a lot job postings for engineers who are supposed to know every computer system ever developed, along with a whole slew of diverse applications. For one thing, no one person is going to have expertise on every type of system in use today. Such a job description actually shows the applicant that you, the employer, don't really know what you're looking for. It also shows that you likely have a very heterogeneous or hodge-podge computer network, and that you expect your engineers to be experts on all the different types of systems. Many excellent candidates will think, "No thanks, I'll pass." Putting too much information about the types of systems an applicant needs to have experience with will also tell hackers a lot about your company's computer network.

INTERVIEWING

No matter how you come into possession of an applicant's resume, double check her background and experiences, as well as her references.

Table 8.4: The International Information Systems Security Certification Consortium (ISC^2) Certifications

CISSP	Certified Information Systems Security Professional	Recognized as the first credential accredited by ANSI to ISO standard 17024.2003 in the field of information Security.
ISSAP	Information Systems Security Architecture Professional	Provides recognition for advanced information security expertise in architecture.
ISSEP	Information Systems Security Engineering Professional	Provides recognition for advanced information security expertise in engineering
ISSMP	Information Systems Security Management Professional	Provides recognition for advanced information security expertise in management

And be sure that the person making the final decision has knowledge of the position to be filled. Since I have a both a technical and a security background, when I conduct interviews for computer jobs, I am able to ask questions specifically based on what an applicant puts on their resume. I am always surprised by how many "senior computer engineers" have little to no knowledge of the simplest computer-related tasks. That's why it's so important to have a technically competent person who knows something about the job conduct the interviews.

Doing so makes it harder for applicants to bluff their way through an interview. It is nonetheless important to check with your company's human resources department about what questions you are allowed to ask applicants during an interview. The interview questions need to be fair, consistent, and relevant to the position being sought. I always ask applicants the same questions. I only vary when asking questions that pertain uniquely to an applicant's resume. As mentioned, I feel that if you've listed a certain skill on your resume, it is fair game to ask you about it during the interview. This turns out to be an effective tool to uncover applicants who greatly overstate their backgrounds and skill sets.

When interviewing information security professionals, questions that you can use to weed out unqualified candidates include:

- Describe what a firewall is, what it does, and the different types.
- What are the different uses of a physical firewall versus a software firewall?
- Describe what encryption is, as well as the differences between symmetric and asymmetric algorithms.
- What is steganography?
- What are the major components of the following governmental regulations: the Gramm-Leach-Bliley Act, California Senate Bill 1386, and Sarbanes-Oxley? (If you're hiring a security professional for to work in the health care industry, include the Health Insurance Portability and Accountability Act.)
- Discuss the concept of two-factor authentication.
- Describe the three different factors of authentication and give examples of each.
- What concepts make up the C.I.A. triad?

As important as "hard" skills are, "soft" skills are just as important. Gauging how an applicant answers the technical questions can give an insight into his ability to clearly and concisely express complex technical issues. This is a skill that is critical to interact successfully with business managers and other non-security personnel. It is also important to get a sense of where an applicant stands on what I've called the security spectrum. On one extreme there lies the "anything goes" attitude, while the other is a Department-of-Defense type rigidity. It is important to know where on the spectrum candidates lie, and how aligned they are with where your company is. While in most private-sector companies, even in the more sensitive areas, I've often said "we're not launching nukes" to express the idea that we don't need to be as absolute about security as the military. A candidate whose thoughts on security vary greatly from your company's will likely not be a good fit.

SEEK OUT THE BEST AND BRIGHTEST

You should always strive to hire the best and the brightest. It takes a certain amount of knowledge in the field that you are recruiting for to recognize that talent. I have seen bad hiring decisions made because nobody involved in the recruitment process had a sufficient depth of knowledge in the particular area. If you don't have a background in technology, don't be the only person involved in the hiring process to bring on a computer engineer. While you may be a good judge of character, and what type of employee a prospective candidate might make, that doesn't mean you can recognize a strong computer engineer. Ensure that at least one person involved on the hiring team is either a current practitioner, or at a minimum has specific knowledge and expertise in the field.

It is also important to check references. What does a candidate's former employer have to say about him? Now, this may be somewhat problematic, as many companies have policies against giving out recommendations, whether positive or negative. If a candidate has a record of frequently changing jobs, or is unable to answer why he wants to leave his current position, consider it a red flag. It is also worth asking other professionals in the field. It truly is a small world. You may be able to find something out about a candidate from colleagues in the field.

We've all seen resumes that were much more impressive than the person whose name was on the top of the first page. Information security is such a new field that one of the challenges in hiring for senior positions is knowing the skill sets to look for. To be truly effective in an information security role, you need to have a background in technology, security, policy, and regulatory compliance. Unless you are a very skilled technical recruiter, you generally need to have specific experience in the field to be able to know what skill sets you are looking for.

Another common mistake that I have seen made in the recruitment process is taking too long to make a decision. When you have found a strong candidate, work quickly in order to bring her on board. The odds are that yours is not the only position she is interviewing for. I have seen many top candidates lost because companies drag their feet in making hiring decisions. A candidate may also have concerns about a company that takes an inordinate amount of time to extend a job offer. She may wonder how effective the management staff is when it takes months to make a hiring decision.

EMPLOYEE RETENTION

Once you've got people hired, you're going to want to retain them. Retention is far less expensive than recruitment. This doesn't mean that you have to pay a person twice the going market salary for their skill set. A competitive wage, while important, is only a part of what keeps employees satisfied with their jobs. Different people are motivated by different things, so no one strategy aimed at increasing retention will work for a large staff. It is incumbent upon management to come up with a comprehensive retention strategy. And it bears repeating—holding onto staff and keeping people happy reduces the chances a disgruntled employee will wreak havoc on his way out the door. Here are some of the retention tools that that have worked for me.

On-Boarding

You need to make people feel welcome and at home from the start. For many new hires, getting an understanding of the corporate culture is one of the biggest initial challenges. Information that old-timers take for granted may be smoke and mirrors to most new employees. Information that the veterans just know from working there for years may not be formally documented anywhere. Providing a new hire with a more seasoned employee to serve as a mentor will help them to assimilate to the corporate culture.

It is also important that you have a formalized on-boarding process for new employees. This includes personnel-related items such as ensuring the first paycheck is right on time, as well ensuring that they are made aware of any company benefits they may be eligible for. What kind of impression would it make if it took weeks to equip your new employee with a laptop, a PDA, and any other standard equipment? It's also important to provide new hires with training in areas such as information security and data handling. Telling them about social issues such as the company dress code and where the break room is will help them feel like they're part of the team. If you just sit the new guy in his cube and forget about him, don't be surprised if you suffer a high degree of turnover.

Communication

One of the most important things for a manager to do is to communicate. I hold weekly meetings with my staff to discuss issues that affect the team. Employees want to know what is going on in the company, especially in areas that affect them directly. Team meetings should not be monologues. Managers need to make a point of giving each team member a chance to bring up any items that he or she wants to talk about.

On a case-by-case basis, I also hold recurring one-on-one meetings with certain members of my team. I generally use this more with remote employees that don't have the opportunity to just walk up to me during the day if they have a question. I also have one-on-one meetings with new hires for a certain amount of time as part of the overall on-boarding process. In addition to being somewhat comforting for new hires, it also gives them a sense of accomplishment when, between the two of us, we decide that they didn't need the meetings any more.

As a manager, don't be afraid to admit that you don't know everything. Obviously nobody has all the answers, and your employees will appreciate your honesty. If you try to fool your employees into thinking you do know everything, they'll spot that in a second. I once had a manager who wouldn't talk to anybody out of fear that he didn't have all the answers. This "management by absentia" style was unbelievably ineffective. In addition to not communicating with the team, this person didn't seek input from anyone on it, either. The combination of no communication and very bad decisions on the part of the manager caused half the team to leave in a four-month period. For many employees, the number one aspect of job satisfaction is the manager they report to. In this particular instance, this manager caused an exodus that eviscerated the team's knowledge base. It took years to recover.

Recognition

If your company has a formal awards program, make sure that you employees are recognized for their hard work. Believe me, it can be hard being a popular security guy. That's because security professionals point out deficiencies in any project that they're assessing. To make matters worse, we then come up with requirements to fix the deficiencies, requirements that will usually cost money and take more time and resources. While it's all in the best interests of the company, it can be a tough sell some times. As a manager, you might have to recognize your employees yourself.

Style

Managers have a large impact on employee job satisfaction. If one of your subordinate managers is experiencing a lot of turnover in their team, you might not have to look too far to determine the cause. I have counseled managers about their interaction with their staff in the following way. If you have a team of 30 people, and two of them don't like you, it's probably just two disgruntled employees. However, if you have a team of 30 people, and 28 of them don't like you, you're the problem.

110   Information Security

While such a concept may personally be hard for some people to accept, the impact that bad managers can have on a company is huge. I have seen entire teams quit out of frustration caused by bad managers. So, senior managers, know what is going on in your teams. Don't limit the communications with your staff to only your direct reports. Make yourself approachable so that your employees will give you honest feedback.

First and foremost, communicate with your staff. If your team never sees you or hears from you, and their only interaction is the occasional e-mail, you'll be seen as a nonentity. Even worse, your employees will feel that they aren't important to you. Some managers don't want to interact with their teams because they are afraid their subordinates might know that they don't know everything. The hard fact is that nobody knows everything. If you pretend that you do, you'll come off as arrogant. You'll also miss out on the opportunity to draw on the talents of your team in those situations where you don't have the answer. Assuming you hired the best and the brightest, they'll actually be a tremendous resource. Your team will appreciate it when you seek their input as appropriate. Don't be afraid to appear human; none of us have all the answers all the time.

BARRIERS TO RETENTION

The Admin-Manager

Many companies hire what can be considered "admin-managers" to be in charge of security. These are people who can track vacation time and manage a budget, but have absolutely no background in technology, data security, or regulatory compliance. This is a very dangerous practice. I am always surprised by the number of people attending security seminars who have no background in the field. Yet many such individuals hold very senior IT security positions in their respective companies. A five-day security seminar is no substitute for years, or ideally decades, of experience in the field. A rule of thumb that I use is, if you can't hold your own when talking with me about any number of issues involved in data security, you shouldn't be a CISO, CSO, or IT Security Director for any large company that deals with non-public information.

I was once asked by a Corporate Information Security Officer what the difference was between SSH and SSL. SSH is secure shell, a secure way to transmit data. SSH is also an interactive protocol. You can tunnel any protocol through it, so it can be a potential security issue depending on how it is deployed. SSL, secure socket layer, is the protocol used to encrypt data while in transit over the Internet. This should be common knowledge to even mid-level engineers and security "experts." To be asked such a question by a senior executive in the data security field was very troubling. Companies that hire admin-managers are exposing themselves to a huge amount of risk. This is particularly true for companies that are bound by any number of state or federal laws and regulations specific to the handling of sensitive personal data.

Decision Makers versus Problem Solvers

I have seen many managers who are decision makers rather than problem solvers. Another risk of hiring admin-managers is that they tend to make decisions to get the issue off their desk. (But this isn't a problem unique to admin-managers alone.) Uninformed decisions can make situations worse, a real problem when dealing with security issues that may have either a legal or a regulatory impact to your company. If the security "gig" is just a step in an admin-manager's career ladder, he may have the mindset of delaying a problem long enough for him to move on to the next position within the company. That's a strong argument for both not hiring admin-managers and not allowing key managers to move around too often.

Constant Re-Organizations

While reorganizations are a part of corporate life, if done in a haphazard manner they can cause serious disruptions. Long-term efforts may be stopped and started numerous times, corresponding to ever-changing personnel at key managerial levels. The more senior a manager is in the organization, the longer they should be expected to stay in a position. As decisions become more strategic, more senior, and more long term, you want to make sure they are followed through. Constant changes in direction are not only disruptive, but they can be bad for morale as well. Employees will see that any vision or direction their team is striving toward will only last for six months to a year until the next reorganization. Fully embracing a vision is difficult if the vision changes every six months. It can also take six months or longer after a re-organization for the dust to settle and to start developing strategic visions. If your company is moving managers around every 12 to 18 months, long-term plans may never be fully implemented.

Don't Be the Smartest Person on Your Team

If as a manager you're the smartest person on your team, you did a very poor job of hiring employees. Seek out the best and brightest, and be secure enough in your own skills to not be intimidated because somebody on your team may know more about some issues than you do. As a manager, I both provide direction to, and seek input from, the members of my team. Since I strive to hire the best and brightest, I get to seek the input of the best and brightest. Believe me, as complex as this field can be, that can actually be very comforting.

AIDS TO RETENTION

Defend Your Staff

There isn't anything more demoralizing than letting somebody on your team catch grief for a well-thought-out, yet incorrect, decision. Situations like that are learning experiences, and provide an opportunity for you to counsel your team members. I have a hard and fast rule, which is a part of my welcoming speech to new hires. I always say that only I can bust their chops. If anybody else tries, they are to come to me, and I will take care of it. I believe that in most instances, an incorrect decision is related to training. Well, guess what, managers: It's our job to ensure that our staff is fully trained. As demoralizing as not defending a team member can be, standing up for a team member can provide a huge morale boost.

Now, this is a two-way street. When I see bad decisions being made, I work quickly to discover if it's a training issue or an attitudinal one. Either issue can be addressed, just in different ways. When it comes to attitudinal issues, I have developed an A-B-C philosophy. "A" employees are self-motivated hard workers, and are what every manager hopes for. "B" employees will do their jobs just fine, but require more managerial oversight. "C" employees take up 90 percent of your time as a manager, and generally do a poor job anyway. I have a simple strategy when dealing with C level employees. I motivate them to become B employees, or I fire them. I have better things to do with my time than to focus 90 percent of my energies on C employees. C employees will also have a negative impact on the rest of your team, who usually have to pick up the slack for their poor performance.

Provide Training

Insufficient training is the other potential cause of poor decision making. Providing training is not only a critical aspect of good decision making, it also aids in retention. Many employees see company-provided training as one of the perks of their position. Factor training costs in as part of your budget. If you don't, you'll be spending that money on recruitment anyway.

People learn in different ways, so no one training method will be appropriate for your entire staff. A comprehensive training program needs to include a combination of books, industry sponsored online seminars, industry seminars, company-sponsored online training, and instructor-led and classroom training. Many companies will have a set of annual training requirements that generally consist of in-house instructor-led training, as well as company-sponsored online training. With a reasonable amount of managerial oversight, employees need to supplement the mandatory training with other learning opportunities that will make them more effective in their jobs, and also further their careers.

Encourage your employees to seek out industry-specific certifications. You can't imagine the morale boost when one of my employees asks me to sign their form attesting that they have the required experience in the security field to become a full CISSP after they've just passed the exam. If a certain training topic is appropriate for your entire team, consider paying to have instructor-led training brought inhouse. Many training companies will send their instructors to you—for a fee, of course. This may actually be cheaper if it saves having your entire team travel to the vendor's training facility.

While security and technical training is more geared to engineers and security staff, a certain level of security awareness should be required for all employees. The protection of sensitive data is not just the job of information security officers. All employees should be made aware of their responsibilities to protect sensitive data, and how to safeguard their laptops, PDAs, and more. Part of the new hire paperwork should include information on network usage, the proper handling of sensitive information, and expectations around protecting company-issued equipment. Regular, ongoing training on security related issues should be a part of an overall awareness program. Information security officers are also a good resource for providing awareness training.

Organizational Considerations

Depending on the size of your organization, you may want to consider having information security officers embedded in the line businesses in addition to your more centralized corporate data security group. Beyond the training aspect, having security officers embedded in this manner will allow them to develop a better knowledge of the inner workings of the business unit. This will help them make decisions better suited for the particular line of business. This type of structure works best with centralized management of the information security staff. It will ensure a more consistent skill set among the security personnel. It's also important to recognize that the skills an information security officer (ISO,) has will vary somewhat depending on the particular area they'll be focusing on.

For example, if an ISO will be working in a group that is in a mainframe environment, beyond a security background, she will need technical knowledge of mainframes. The same will hold true for other technical areas such as networking, Windows, mid-range systems, UNIX, etc. Since the risk is with the data, knowing the risks specific to the various technologies is critical to be an effective ISO. A one-size-fits-all approach does not work.

Centralized management of the information security personnel that are embedded directly in business units also frees them from undue influences. Sometimes it can be difficult to give an unfavorable risk rating to your direct manager's pet project. I recommend that when information security professionals are embedded directly in a line of business that they have at least a dotted-line reporting structure up to a senior level corporate security officer for the given company.

SECURITY IN THE ORGANIZATIONAL HIERARCHY

At an organizational level, it is best for the head of security to be very high up in the corporate hierarchy. Your company's most senior security officer should be a "C" level executive. The chief security officer needs to be at the same level as the chief technology officer. This is important because, at times, the needs of production can be at odds with security requirements. It's also why a company's security division should be separate from the group whose charter is strictly technology and production support. Back in my engineering days, I could get a new server up and running in less than an hour, which pleased users. However, a properly configured and fully patched system would take longer. The extra time was taken up by things such as making sure the system had the appropriate patches applied, ensuring that any unnecessary services were shut off, and more. Doing something right, with security in mind, can often take some extra time and effort on the front end. The upfront costs are offset by having a more secure system that in most cases is also more reliable as well. By properly positioning your company's security division within the overall organizational structure, such concerns will get the appropriate level of attention.

It can also be very demoralizing to security personnel to be constantly overruled in the name of expediency. There is a give and take between the need to get systems into production and the concerns of security. Such competing interests need to be discussed on equal footing. If production constantly trumps security, your security experts will move on to other companies.

Employees at all levels of your company are the heart and soul of your organization. If you hire the best and treat them well, you'll reap rewards for years to come. The opposite, of course, is also true, which can have lasting effects on a company.

CHAPTER 9

CONTRACTUAL CONSIDERATIONS

An organization engaging in business relationships with other companies is very common. Companies often go to third parties to provide a wide range of products and services. The actual services that a third party can provide are nearly limitless. To keep with the general overall theme of this book, I will focus on services that involve access to your company's network and data, such as off-site data storage, remote production support, outsourced call center support, and software development. When conducting contract negotiations to enter into a business relationship with a third party, there's more to consider than what they're going to charge you for their product or service.

It is also worth noting that just as a "general" computer support engineer likely does not have the same skill sets as a security engineer, most attorneys are not computer security experts. Very specific disciplines are required to make certain that all necessary ground is covered in contracts that deal with sensitive electronic data. So, the team that your company puts together to work through contractual issues in addition to a contracts attorney should also include an information security professional as well as a compliance officer.

NON-DISCLOSURE AGREEMENTS

In the intertwined business world that we live in today, third parties will get access to your company's sensitive data. This can include information about your customers, or your company's latest market strategy. Have specific non-disclosure language in your contract dictating that any information that they gain from their relationship with you is not to be shared with any outside parties. You do not want your customer lists sold to your competitors. If you just paid a million dollars to a company to conduct a

market study for you, do you really want it selling the results to other companies? You would not want your survey company to sell the results of
your customer reactions to a product that you sell, or to fee structures that
you are considering changing, or to a brand new marketing campaign.

Business strategies that your company is considering undertaking
should be considered sensitive data as well, and any third parties that
are involved should be required to sign non-disclosure agreements. Keep
in mind that this includes the print shop that is designing your marketing
brochures to launch your latest business campaign. Sensitive data is not
limited to customer information and market strategies. If your CEO just
submitted an insurance claim to cover the cost of her teenager's alcohol
rehabilitation, you certainly would not want that information disclosed
to anybody. While a disclosure of this type would likely be in violation
of numerous data privacy laws, with non-disclosure language, it would
also constitute a breach of contract. This would give your company
specific recourse as outlined in the contract.

SECURITY LANGUAGE

If the organization that you are doing business with will either store or
have access to your company's sensitive data, having specific security
language in the contract is critical. If you are comfortable with the security
controls that your company abides by, then you should insist that any third
parties that will house your sensitive data have similar controls. The contract should contain specific language mandating the security controls that
are expected to be in place to protect your company's sensitive data. Have
the third party provide you with the results of any independent security
reviews that they have performed during the year. Some common ones
include a Financial Institutions Shared Assessment Program (FISAP) and
a Statement of Audit Standards-70 (SAS-70). A Type I SAS-70 looks at how
appropriate a set of controls are, while the Type II actually performs testing
against the stated controls. The FISAP was developed to establish a set of
agreed upon standards for security audits of financial institutions by BITS.
Learn more at www.bitsinfo.org/FISAP/index.php. The SAS-70 was
developed by the American Institute of Certified Public Accounts (AICPA).
More information about the SAS-70 can be found at www.aicpa.org. If your
company has an internal team that performs third-party security assessments, ensure such reviews are clearly outlined in the contract.

SECURITY REVIEWS

The Big 4 auditing firms all provide security audits. There are a number
of other companies in the market today that will provide similar services
as well. If your company has its own team of engineers that can perform

these types of reviews, all the better. Notice that I have switched from the term auditor to engineer. An auditor can review security policies and determine if they are in compliance with any applicable laws and regulations. It takes somebody with an engineering skill set to actually verify if the technical controls outlined in a policy are actually being utilized. A company can have a policy that states they encrypt sensitive data. Verifying that encryption is actually being used to protect your company's sensitive data is a different matter altogether.

FOURTH-PARTY AGREEMENTS

Is the company that you are outsourcing a particular service to merely acting as a middle-man and having yet another company perform the work? Are they even required to advise you if they outsource the work to another party that you've contracted them to provide? Such a fourth-party arrangement, as I call it, can have both financial as well as security implications. From a financial perspective, if the company that you've contracted with to perform a certain service is merely a middle-man, you're most likely paying more for the service than you should be. You are paying their markup if they are having another company perform the actual work.

In situations like this, you most likely would not have any kind of business relationship with the fourth-party company. Perhaps even more troubling would be the security implications. What security controls does the fourth-party company utilize to protect your sensitive data? Will it be selling your data? Is the company located in the same country your company is incorporated in? Do you know if your data is being sent to fourth-party companies located in countries such as India, Mexico, Russia, China, Singapore, or Pakistan? Don't find out that your sensitive data is being sent overseas by learning of a security breach of the company on the evening newscast.

If you do not want your third-party companies to outsource the services that you have contracted with them to provide to other companies, include specific language forbidding it in the contract. If you don't want your data to leave the county, clearly say so in the contract.

BACKGROUND CHECKS

Require companies that will have access to your sensitive data perform background checks on their employees. As with many points in contract negotiations, this may be a point of contention. They will likely want to perform background checks only on employees that have access to sensitive data, and not on lower-level employees. This is a risk tolerance decision that you are going to have to make. As was discussed in Chapter 8, a common hacker trick is to gain access to sensitive areas while bypassing most background checks and security screenings by seeking out low-level positions. Include language that will require the third party to perform background checks on their employees, as well as any vendor personnel or sub-contractors that they may utilize. Ensure that the precise nature of the background checks are compliant with any laws or regulations specific to either your industry, or the counties that you're located in. An example would be the Patriot Act in the United States. Some examples of what to look for when conducting a background check include:

- Felony convictions,
- Misdemeanor convictions that involve acts of dishonesty such as fraud or theft,
- Illegal drug use, and
- Bankruptcies.

If you are a government or military agency, or a company that contracts with such organizations, security clearances may be required as a condition of hire. Secret, top-secret, and even more sensitive types of clearances involve very comprehensive background checks.

NONCITIZENS

If you want your third party to only employ people who are citizens of the country in which your company is located, then say so in the contract. Legal residents and temporary workers who hold visas do not necessarily have to be excluded. Insist that your third-party companies validate the legal status of any non-citizens that they choose to employ. Illegal immigration is a serious problem in the United States. Consider that every undocumented immigrant has already violated at least one law just by coming into the country illegally. Many also commit crimes such as identity theft, perjury, and providing either forged or stolen documents in order to gain employment. Do you want to accept the risk to having people that have already committed a handful of felony crimes to have access to your company's sensitive data?

INSURANCE

Depending on the nature of the company that you're dealing with, and the specifics of the engagement itself, you should insist that it carry certain types of insurance coverage. Some different types of insurance coverage that are common include the following:

- Commercial general liability/umbrella insurance providing coverage for premises-operation liability, products-completed operations liability, independent-contractors liability, personal and advertising, and contractual liability covering all vendor personnel engaged in the performance of services hereunder.

- Professional liability insurance covering vendor and vendor personnel.
- Internet liability insurance, including unauthorized access, unauthorized use, theft of data, virus transmission, denial of service, personal injury, advertising injury, failure to protect privacy, and intellectual property infringement. The language should cover the liability of third party and the liability of "client company" arising out of the design and development of the systems used to operate and maintain the services.
- Automobile/umbrella liability insurance, covering vendor personnel.

The actual dollar amount of the insurance coverage for the various types of issues is dependent on several factors. These include the nature of the business engagement as well as the size of the respective companies. The more risk that your company could potentially be exposed to, the higher the insurance coverage that you'd want the third party to carry. Large companies need to seriously consider the risks of having much smaller companies perform tasks that could potentially expose them to extraordinarily high amounts of risk.

Consider the following scenario. A small company has just suffered a data breach, and 500,000 records of your customers' information has just been stolen. The potential financial loss of such a breach can be well over $15,000,000. A company with a net worth of $5,000,000 that carries a $1,000,000 liability policy cannot possibly cover such a loss. In such a scenario, the liability language contained in the contract may well be reduced to mere words on a piece of paper. The old adage of "you can't get blood from a turnip" applies to this situation. This is not to say that larger companies should not do business with smaller ones. Just be very careful with the nature of the engagement, and the type of access that they are given to your data as well as your network assets.

NOTIFICATION OF A SECURITY BREACH

Include specific language in the contract requiring third parties to notify you in the event of a security breach that either did, or potentially could, involve a loss of your sensitive data. Include specific timelines, generally within 24 to 48 hours. You want to be notified right away to be able determine the appropriate course of action to take. Insist that your company be notified before the media is called. You don't want to find out that your customer data may have been breached at a vendor site by hearing about it on television. Depending on local laws and regulations, you may have to settle for being notified second—after law enforcement.

RIGHT TO TERMINATE THE CONTRACT

Both parties to a contract should be able to terminate the agreement under certain conditions. It is common to require written notice of the intent to terminate a contract, with a pre-determined lead time. Early termination fees and any refunds should also be clearly spelled out in the contract. At the end of the business relationship, whether or not it's related to an early termination, ensure that you get all of your data and assets back. Require the third party to either return the electronic data to you, or delete it in such a way that it cannot be recovered. Remember that the devil is in the details. Consider the fact that data that could be on paper, on servers, on backup tapes, or on CDs as well as on other types of removable storage devices.

ACTIONS UPON THE TERMINATION OF A BUSINESS RELATIONSHIP

When you terminate a business relationship with a third party, there are certain actions that must be taken from a security perspective. These need to be written into the contract so they can be agreed upon in advance. All of your company's sensitive data must be returned or irretrievably destroyed. "Degaussing" is a termed used to refer to the process of making data that's stored on magnetic media irretrievable. Insist on that language in your contract. If a company merely deletes your sensitive data, it is still on the computer. In most cases, deleting merely moves the data to an unused portion of the hard drive that can easily be retrieved. Also be aware of the fact that your data can be on servers, backup tapes, CDs, or a whole slew of other devices. If that data is critical to you, insist that it is either returned or irretrievably destroyed.

Any access the third party has to your computer systems or your physical facilities should be removed as well. This means deactivating access badges and deleting computer access accounts. Make it part of your "decoupling" process to ensure eliminating such access doesn't fall through the cracks.

A general theme throughout this book has been the importance of getting input from highly qualified security professionals. When it comes to contracts, you'd obviously want to engage an attorney that specializes in contracts law. With that said, don't be too quick to leave the security professional or the compliance expert out of the negotiations. While not attorneys, they are experts on the intricacies of data security and regulatory compliance, both of which need to be accounted for throughout the development of the contract.

CHAPTER 10

DATA PRIVACY LAWS

Why do various organizations have data security programs? The answer depends to an extent on the nature of the data they possess, and more importantly their attitudes towards data privacy. Governmental intelligence agencies, as well a country's military organizations, have stringent data-privacy rules for obvious national security reasons. Private-sector companies spend a lot of time and effort protecting data about the next-generation gadget that is soon to be released, or the secret formula of their popular soft drink products. The driving force there is to protect the highly valued secret. However, most companies that have formal data privacy programs to protect customer data do so only because there are various governmental regulations requiring them to. The policies they use to protect customer private information generally fall short of those protecting the next gadget that may be worth millions. Rare is the company that safeguards sensitive consumer data out of moral reasons—because they believe it's the right thing to do.

When the private sector doesn't act responsibly, the public sector will regulate its behavior. The lack of appropriate stewardship of sensitive information is certainly no exception. The vast majority of the data-privacy laws in existence today have come about as a result of numerous high profile data breaches. The data breach that ChoicePoint suffered in 2005 is widely referenced as an argument for the need for strong government oversight. Interestingly enough, according to public documents, the ChoicePoint data breach involved approximately 140,000 records. In 2006, the United States Veterans Affairs suffered a data breach that involved roughly 26.5 million records.

While trying not to focus too much on what could be characterized as a "do as I say not as I do" perspective, the reality is that data-privacy laws are here to stay. With each passing year, new laws come into play requiring more controls and carrying different penalties. If I were to put a positive spin on the immergence of these laws, I would liken it to the phenomena that the computer industry saw in the late 1990s. Most companies spent a lot of time and effort upgrading both their computer hardware and software in preparation for the new millennium. The reason was simple: they feared that their older systems would malfunction in one way or another on January 1, 2000. While many of the concerns never materialized, companies realized the performance benefits of modernizing their computer systems. The same can be said for today's focus on data security. A side benefit of companies trying to become compliant with data privacy laws is that customers will see their sensitive information being better protected.

RAMIFICATIONS OF A DATA BREACH

It is important to understand the impact that a data breach can have on your company. When I received a letter from the office of Veterans Affairs (VA) notifying me of the data breach, there was little I could do. I couldn't decide that I no longer wanted to be a veteran of the United States military. So, while the breach was undoubtedly embarrassing for the VA, there was no real monetary loss, or a great exodus of its customer base.

On the other hand, the risk to private sector companies is far more serious. Industry estimates put the expense of a breach of sensitive customer information to be anywhere from $35 up to a staggering $140 per record, according to the Ponemon Institute. The variance depends on the particulars, including the nature of the data that was lost, fines associated with any applicable laws, credit monitoring expenses, legal fees, loss of customer confidence, etc. Even at the low end, $35 per record, few companies would survive the expense of a security breach of 26.5 million records, which by that measure would carry a price tag of a whopping $927,500,000. Loss of customer confidence and trust is perhaps most troubling for companies. By their nature, certain companies can't survive without customers willing to entrust their personal information with them. Banks, credit unions, insurance companies, and others need to be keenly aware of such a risk. Loss of trust because of its involvement in the Enron scandal drove Arthur Anderson, one of the Big 5 accounting firms, out of business. Keep these facts and figures in mind the next time there's a decision to be made whether or not your company can afford to integrate security into your overall business model. Depending on the nature of the business you're in, the answer may be simple: You can't afford not to.

NON-PUBLIC DATA THAT IS IN THE PUBLIC RECORD

Consider the amount of personal information that is freely available from various county government offices around the United States.

Whether it's local, county, state, or federal, many government offices have sensitive personal information about all of us readily available. Documents such as property records, death certificates, and divorce decrees are all public record, and most contain data that under law would be considered non-public personal information. Many are available for a small fee at various government offices, while some can be viewed over the Internet. Some states have begun to pass laws requiring that sensitive personal information be removed from certain documents. There is no uniformity in this area, as different state laws focus on different public documents. It is also doubtful that government agencies would consider the data privacy laws to be retroactive, and remove sensitive data from public documents that pre-dated the governing statute.

Ironically, the lack of uniformity gets even worse when you consider that approximately a dozen states that have data-breach notification laws apply them only to the private sector, while giving their own agencies a pass.

VARIANCES AMONG STATE LEVEL DATA-BREACH DISCLOSURE LAWS

There is greater variance when it comes to the data-breach disclosure laws of the various states within the United States. The specific data elements that are considered sensitive is another example. Most states pattern their data breach laws after California Senate Bill 1386, which passed in 2003. That landmark data-breach law defines personal information as an individual's first name or first initial and last name in combination with one or more of the following elements:

- Social Security Number,
- Driver's license number or California Identification Card number, and
- Account number, debit card, or credit card number, in combination with any required information such as an access code or a password that would grant access to an individual's financial account.

The law does provide an exemption to the disclosure requirement if the stolen data was encrypted. Both the name and the other elements must be encrypted for this exemption to apply.

Other states have subtle differences in what data they cover. For example, Kansas Senate Bill 196 requires disclosure whether or not any required security code was included in the breach of a financial account number or credit or debit card account number. Remember, encryption is not synonymous with data privacy. This is particularly true if, in addition to customer information being hacked, the encryption keys used to protect the data were stolen as well. Pennsylvania Senate Bill 712 makes specific mention of this fact. It requires disclosure of customer information if the breach includes encryption keys, or if the breach involved a person who had access to them.

Beyond the encryption element, many states' data-breach notification laws provide an exemption to disclosure if the data was redacted. (Redacting is when sensitive data is altered in some way—for example, only providing the last four digits of a person's Social Security Number.) The lesson here would be not to use sensitive data in its raw form unless it is absolutely necessary. Many laws also say that if upon investigation it is deemed unlikely that the stolen data will be misused, then the company doesn't need to disclosure the fact that it had a security breach. The laws do not provide any real guidance in this area as to what facts would be required to make such a determination. There is also a real conflict of interest for a company that has just suffered a data breach to be able to determine unilaterally that the misuse of the stolen data was unlikely to occur. At a minimum of $35 per record, there's a strong motivation to determine that the stolen information won't be misused. This is particularly true if the determination is based solely a company's impression of the hacker's intent when stealing the data. Trying to make such a determination is not only very difficult, if not impossible, but it also most likely would not stand up to the light of public scrutiny if the facts surrounding the data breach were to get out. A company could very well find itself trying to handle the fallout of a perceived cover-up, in addition to the issue of a data breach. If you're going to determine that the misuse of stolen data is unlikely, make it for technical reasons. Make sure the technical reasons are valid, and can be explained in a way that the public can understand.

Some states even require that sensitive data on paper be handled securely. Those laws specifically mention shredding as a way to securely dispose of sensitive data that's on paper.

Table 10.1 provides a handy matrix of information on data-breach disclosure laws of the various states.

SOCIAL SECURITY NUMBERS AND CREDIT/DEBIT CARD ACCOUNT NUMBERS

Another area where the laws of the individual states vary is protecting data such as Social Security numbers and credit/debit card account numbers. Social Security numbers are considered very sensitive, and are covered by the various states' data breach laws. Many states have enacted additional laws that specifically prohibit placing Social Security numbers on a wide range of documents. Some of these include employee paychecks, a candidate's nomination papers, membership/club cards, health insurance cards, drivers licenses, etc. Many laws include both

Table 10.1: Data Breach Disclosure Laws

State	Statute	Covered Entities **B=Business** **G=Government**	Covered Media **E=Electronic** **P=Physical**	Exemptions to Disclosure **E=Encrypted** **R=Redacted** **M=Misuse unlikely**
AL	SB 114	B	E	E
AR	SB 1167	B, G	E, P	E, R
AZ	SB 1338	B, G	E	E, R
CA	SB 1386	B, G	E	E
CO	HB 1119	B	E	E, M
CT	SB 650	B, G	E	E, M
DC	28 DCC §§ 3851 et seq.	B	E	E
DE	HB 116	B, G	E	E, M
FL	HB 481	B, G	E	E
GA	SB 230	B	E	E, R
HI	SB 2290	B, G	E	E, M, R
ID	SB 1374	B, G	E	E, M
IL	HB 1633	B, G	E, P	E
IN	SB 503	B, G	E	E, R
KS	SB 196	B, G	E	E, R, M
LA	SB 205	B, G	E	E, M
MA	HB 4144	B, G	E, P	E
MD	HB 208	B	E	E, M
ME	LD 1671	B	E	E
MN	SF 2118	B	E	E
MT	HB 732	B	E,P	E
MI	SB 309	B, G	E	E, M, R
NC	HB 1048 & 1248	B, G	E, P	E, R
ND	SB 2251	B	E	E, R*
NE	LB 876	B, G	E	E, M

State	Statute	Covered Entities	Covered Media	Exemptions to Disclosure
NH	HB 1660	B, G	E	E, M
NV	NRS 603A.220	B, G	E	E, M
NJ	AB 4001	B, G	E	E, M
NY	AB 4254	B,G	E	E
OH	HB 104	B, G	E	E, R, M
OK	HB 2357	G	E	E
OR	SB 583	B	E, P	E, M
PA	SB 712	B, G	E	E, R
RI	H6191	B, G	E	E, M
TN	HB 2170	B, G	E	E, M
TX	HB 698	B	P	R
UT	HB 69	B	E, P	E, M
VT	SB 284	B	E	E, M, R
WA	SB 6043	B, G	E	E
WI	Act 138	B, G	E	E, R, M
*Does not specifically use "redaction," but uses terms like "unreadable" and "unusable."				

Social Security numbers of U.S. citizens, as well as Taxpayer Identifications numbers (TINs), which the government assigns temporarily to non-U.S. citizens.

Many companies have long used Social Security numbers as the primary way to identify their customers. In such instances, it would very likely take a large commitment of resources to rework all the applications and databases to use a different identifier. Here again, executives are faced with a business decision. Accept the risk of using Social Security numbers strictly as a reference number, and the penalties if that data is breached, or spend the money that it will take to come up with an alternative. Some companies are developing what can be known as customer identification numbers. A customer identification number (CIN) can provide the same level of referential integrity, one unique CIN per customer, but isn't considered as sensitive under the various data privacy laws as a Social Security number.

Account numbers of both credit and debit cards are also considered very sensitive. Thieves love stealing credit/debit card account information, because they can buy just about anything anywhere. If, in addition to the account number, the fraudsters can steal the expiration date and any associated security number the many cards have, they can shop online with nearly total anonymity.

SIMILARITIES AMONG STATE-LEVEL DATA BREACH DISCLOSURE LAWS

All of the states that have data breach laws hold the data owner liable for disclosure if sensitive data either is stolen or thought to have been stolen. Many companies will send sensitive data to third parties for them to perform some outsourced process of off-site storage. In such instances, if the third party suffers a breach, their liability is strictly to notify the data owner. That would be the company that gave them the data in the first place. The data owner is still liable to notify the affected customers of the data breach itself. While specific language can be placed in a contract requiring the third party to protect the data to a level acceptable to your company, you still may not be fully protected. Consider the fact that most attorneys are not data security experts.

Strong language in a contract is no substitute for an independent on-site assessment of a third party's data security practices. Even if such a contract held the third party liable for all fines associated with a data breach, depending on the number of records involved, the potential loss could be more than the entire net worth of the company itself. Large companies should seriously consider the risks associated with sending millions of their customer records to small companies. You can't sue your outsourced processor with a net worth of $10 million for the $100 million of liability it just cost your company as a result of a data breach.

Credit bureaus such as Experian, Equifax, and TransUnion are an exception to this rule. When companies send data to the credit bureaus, they are deemed to be the data owner. If one of the credit bureaus were to suffer a data breach, they would own disclosure liabilities. This exception for companies that send the credit bureaus sensitive data is not absolute. While there is no strong case law on this yet, conventional legal opinion is that the exception would be specific to why a company sent a bureau the data in the first place. If the information that was provided was part of the normal reporting function of a credit bureau, then the bureaus themselves would be deemed to be the owner of the data. However, some companies will send a credit bureau information for other purposes. Analytics and other statistical modeling are common. In such instances, the original company may still be considered to be the data owner, and be held liable for a breach of that specific data that occurred at the credit bureau.

Another obvious exception is when the private sector is required to send sensitive data to the government. For example, companies can't decide not to send non-public personal information to the Internal Revenue Service if they have concerns with how the IRS protects such data while in their possession. The private sector is also not in a position to require the IRS to permit them to perform an on-site assessment of their security policies and practices. However, they absolutely own the data, as well as any fallout that may occur if they were to suffer a security breach.

ONE STANDARD TO FOLLOW

There are conflicting opinions about whether or not a single standard concerning data privacy and disclosure would make things easier on businesses in developing appropriate security and data handling policies. Even if the federal government were to pass a data privacy law specific to this area, it may not necessarily trump all the laws of the various states. Such a federal law might not include a specific preemption clause. It may merely set a minimum standard, leaving the states to decide individually if they want to be more restrictive.

The closest thing that there is to a single federal standard is the *Interagency Guidance on Response Programs for Security Breaches.* It was jointly issued by the Board of Governors of the Federal Reserve System, the Office of the Comptroller of the Currency, the Office of Thrift Supervision, and the Federal Deposit Insurance Corporation on March 23, 2005. Additional information can be found on the Web site of the Office of the Comptroller of the Currency at www.occ.treas.gov/consumer/Customernoticeguidance.pdf. The standard requires financial institutions have procedures to notify customers about incidents of unauthorized access to customer information that could result in substantial harm or inconvenience to the customer. The provision also requires that the financial institution perform an investigation to promptly determine the likelihood that the information has been or will be misused. If, upon investigation, it is determined that the information either has been misused, or misuse is likely to occur, the affected customers should be notified as soon as possible. The interagency guidance also requires that the primary federal regulator be notified of the breach, whether or not the institution notifies its customers.

DATA PRIVACY LAWS—EUROPEAN UNION

Great Britain has the Data Protection Act (DPA) of 1998, which provides for the privacy and protection of the private data of persons living in the United Kingdom. The act places both requirements and limitations on organizations that collect or hold data and that can identify a person living in the United Kingdom. The Act does not apply to what can be considered private use—for example, keeping a contact list of personal friends on your PDA.

Data collected by any person or organization may only be used for the actual purposes for which the data was collected. Personal data may also only be retained for an appropriate length of time, and may not be disclosed without the expressed consent of the data owner. People who have their data held have the right to:

- View the data that companies have on them. Companies may charge a small fee, which is known as a "subject access" fee;
- Request that information they believe to be inaccurate be corrected; and
- Request not to receive direct marketing solicitations.

Eight principles of the U.K. 1998 Data Privacy Law are:

- Companies shall ensure that personal data is processed both fairly and lawfully;
- Companies shall ensure that personal data shall be obtained only for specified and lawful purposes, and nothing else;
- Companies shall ensure that personal data shall be specific to the stated lawful purpose, and that it is not excessive. In other words, don't request more data than is needed;
- Companies shall ensure that the personal data they have is both accurate and kept up to date as necessary;
- Companies shall only retain the personal data for as long as is necessary for the purposes for which it was originally obtained;
- Companies shall ensure that personal data is processed in compliance with this act;
- Companies shall ensure that appropriate technical and organizational safeguards are in place to protect the data against unauthorized or unlawful access; as well as against its accidental loss or destruction, and to protect the integrity of personal data; and
- Companies shall not permit personal data to be transferred to a country or territory outside the European Economic Area unless said country or territory has adequate levels of data protection.

FEDERAL DATA PRIVACY LAWS IN THE UNITED STATES

Let's cover some of the major data privacy laws within the United States. While this list is not all-inclusive, these are the major laws that many private-sector companies are bound to follow.

The Gramm-Leach-Bliley Act (GLBA), also known as the Financial Services Modernization Act of 1999, provides limited privacy protections against the sale of private financial information. Prior to GLBA, insurance companies, banks, and brokers were all separate. If these companies were to merge, however, they would have the ability to consolidate all personal data, and would be able to cross-sell among their different product offerings. This could result in customers receiving unwanted solicitations for banking products, for instance, that are from the same company that they have insurance with. Due to this issue, the GLBA included three requirements to protect a customer's personal data: First of all, financial institutions, brokerage companies, and insurance companies must protect their customers' personal financial information. Secondly, they must advise their customers of their policies regarding the sharing of your personal financial information. Finally, they must provide customers with the option to opt out of some sharing of their personal financial information. In short, GLBA gives consumers that right to opt out from companies using their personal data for the purpose of cross-selling other products. Additionally, the GLBA codifies protections against pretexting, the practice of obtaining personal information through false pretenses.

The Sarbanes-Oxley Act of 2002, also known as SOX, was passed in response to a number of major corporate accounting scandals involving companies such as Enron and Tyco International. SOX established a level of accountability for publicly traded companies. Corporate executives are now held liable, in some cases personally, for the accuracy of their company's financial accounting and reporting.

The Payment Card Industry (PCI) Data Security Standard (DSS) establishes a common set of industry tools to help ensure the safe handling of sensitive information. It was created as a cooperative effort between both Visa and MasterCard. The PCI standards include both technical requirements for the secure storage, processing, and transmission of cardholder data, and also provisions for testing the methodologies for auditing and scanning procedures.

For doctors, hospitals, insurance companies, and pharmacies, there's the Health Insurance Portability and Accountability Act (HIPAA) of 1996. HIPAA requires that companies have a set of policies to protect individuals' heath records. If your company sends health records to a third party, you are required to ensure that they follow HIPAA guidelines as well. An important point that needs to be made here is that the health insurance records that your company may have about its employees would be covered by HIPAA as well. In short, you don't have to be in the medical field to have medical information covered by HIPAA.

Publicly supported colleges and universities, as well as public grade schools and high schools, are covered by a privacy law known as the Family Educational Rights and Privacy Act (FERPA). FERPA is a federal law designed to protect the privacy of student education records. The law gives parents certain rights with respect to their children's education records. These rights transfer to students when they reach the age of 18 or attend a school beyond the high school level.

Parents or eligible students have the right to inspect and review the student's education records that are maintained by the school. They also have the right to request that a school correct any records they believe to be inaccurate or misleading. If the school decides not to amend the record, the parents then have a right to a formal hearing. After the hearing, if the school still decides not to amend the record, the parents have the right to place a statement with the record saying that they contest the accuracy of the information.

FERPA requires that schools have written permission from the parent in order to release any information from a student's education record. However, the law does allow schools to disclose those records, without consent, to the following parties or under the following conditions:

- School officials with legitimate educational interest;
- A school that a student is transferring to;
- As required for audit or evaluation purposes;
- As required for financial aid purposes;
- To an organization for accrediting purposes;
- In response to a judge's subpoena;
- To appropriate officials in cases of health and safety emergencies; and
- As required by either state or local authorities, within a juvenile justice system.

Schools may disclose, without consent, "directory" information such as a student's name, address, telephone number, date and place of birth, honors and awards, and dates of attendance. However, the schools must notify the parents in advance and give them the opportunity to opt out. Schools are required to notify parents of their rights under FERPA on an annual basis. However, the actual means of notification (special letter, inclusion in a PTA bulletin, student handbook, or newspaper article) are left to the individual school.

TOO MUCH DATA PRIVACY

I normally take a pro-data-privacy stance. But I feel that there are times where data sharing is required, particularly in areas such as public safety and national security. I say this as the United Stated federal government is currently considering several sweeping data privacy laws. In the shadow of the recent tragedy of the Virginia Tech shootings, I submit that Cho Seung-Hui, by virtue of his documented mental health problems, should have been barred from purchasing a firearm. Consider the lives that might have been spared if a warning flag would have come up when he tried to purchase his weapons. The information wouldn't necessarily have to say why he was ineligible to purchase a firearm—just that he was.

That a person who is forbidden from purchasing firearms is trying to do so should in and of itself send a notification to the authorities. In my view, there is such a thing as too much data privacy.

An appropriate amount of data sharing needs to be encouraged to combat other types of activities as well. Financial institutions need to be able to share information about people who are going from bank to bank committing fraudulent acts. Government and law enforcement authorities need to be alerted when somebody is wiring money out of the country from numerous different bank accounts. And as a parent, I would want my school district to know when somebody applying for a job has just been convicted of a crime against children in another state. Responsible data sharing is an important tool to help combat fraudulent and at times even dangerous activities. Just as rats scatter when bright lights are shined on them, criminals also prefer to operate in the shadows. In the rush to ensure data privacy, we must be careful not to create a haven for those who would do us harm.

CHAPTER 11

OVERSEAS OUTSOURCING

Overseas outsourcing is quickly becoming a very popular way for companies to realize cost savings. The obvious reason is that the salaries in countries such as India and Pakistan are generally a fraction of those for workers with comparable skills in countries such as the United States and Great Britain. When conducting an outsourcing cost-benefit analysis and figuring out how much money you'll be saving, keep in mind that there are a number of issues that need to be taken into consideration.

From a logistical perspective, managing operations located in a foreign country can be very complicated. There are many issues to consider just by the nature of having operations located overseas. From a coordination perspective, it is important to keep in mind that when it's day time here in the United States, it's night time in India. That makes scheduling conference calls to discuss strategies somewhat difficult. Facilities based overseas are likely to take longer to recover from a system outage. Any company that had ever had a critical system suffer hardware failure knows that it can be difficult to have a replacement part delivered quickly. This is particularly true when the failed piece of hardware is very expensive, and hence not widely stocked. Consider how that problem might be compounded by having the failed critical system located in a country like Pakistan or India. How quickly will the manufacturer be able to ship the part? Is the required engineering talent on-site at your overseas facility to replace the failed part, or will you have to arrange for an engineer to be brought in as well? Also bear in mind that many server and networking hardware components commonly available here in the United States may be hard to replace overseas.

Any on-site audits or security reviews that you may be required to perform will be much more costly and take longer when the facility is located overseas. You'll have passport and visa issues, not to mention having to take a series of required inoculations. In the current state of world affairs, traveling to countries such as India and Pakistan may also expose your employees to a higher degree of personal risk as well.

And then there are the data security issues. While many companies are sending a wide range of work involving very sensitive data overseas, in most cases they are keeping such activity rather quiet. For example, few companies will openly admit to the public that they send your personal data overseas. The truth is, however, that this is a rather common practice. Many companies will send data overseas due to the reduced costs of processing it. For example, a number of tax preparation companies send your tax records overseas. The actual tax returns are prepared off-shore, with the domestic company merely checking the work. Of course, companies aren't going to openly disclose something like that. If it's mentioned at all, it will likely be buried in the middle of a disclosure statement written in very small type. This is because companies are keenly aware of the public's growing awareness of data-privacy issues, and know that their decisions to send their data overseas might not be well received. The specter of alienating a certain percentage of your customer base needs to be factored in when performing the cost-benefit analysis, and deciding what work to send off-shore. Conversely, would there be public relations value in touting that your company does not send customer sensitive data off-shore? The best decisions are always well informed ones. These realities need to be factored in, because there is much more to consider than the hourly wage of the off-shore workers as compared to their domestic counterparts.

Consider the products of many of the large financial institutions operating in the United States, including checking accounts, savings accounts, CDs, mortgages, home equity loans, and much more. At any given time, each of them will be offering specials for many of the products that they sell. For many people, it is the level of customer service that can have the biggest impact. Are the tellers friendly, does my personal banker make recommendations that are in my best interest, do I get a smile when I walk into the branch?

Here in the twenty-first century, the issue that is just as important as customer service is the security of customer data. If your customers have strong doubts that your bank will keep their personal data secure, then they will likely take their business somewhere else. Consider the public relations advantage for the financial institution that launches a nationwide campaign stating that the security of their customers personal financial data is so important that they don't send it off-shore. Unlike the one-quarter percentage point increase in a CD rate, that is something that your competitors would have a hard time matching.

SENDING SENSITIVE DATA OFF-SHORE

Some of the work being sent overseas includes medical billing records, tax preparations, technical support (call centers), application development, and even server support. This means that a lot of sensitive information—including medical records, financial data, and Social Security numbers—are being sent overseas. India is the number one overseas provider of technical services to companies based in the United States. A word of caution: Remember, you might be outsourcing the work, but in most cases you're not outsourcing the liability for misuse. That you still own.

The National Outsourcing Association, www.noa.co.uk, is a resource for British companies considering using off-shore resources. U.K. law gives its citizens ownership of the personal data maintained by companies. These laws empower U.K. citizens to challenge the accuracy of the data that companies have about them. Great Britain also has strict controls pertaining to sending personal information about its citizens to other countries. Back in 1998, both Great Britain and the European Union passed comprehensive privacy legislation. Among other things, the law requires that transfers of personal data take place only to non-EU countries that provide an "adequate" level of privacy protection.

In contrast, many companies in the United States send non-public personal information overseas without advising their customers. While there are currently no laws against this, the practice could cause regulatory as well as customer-relations issues in the event of a security breach, or even unintended media disclosure.

There have been well-publicized accounts of security issues involved in off-shoring. In 2003, a woman in Pakistan performing clerical work for the UCSF Medical Center threatened to post patients' medical records on the Internet unless she was paid more money. In 2006, HSBC had customer data passed onto fraudsters by a employee of an offshore data-processing center in Bangalore, India. While there are responsible ways to realize savings by using low-cost overseas personnel, many companies outsource in a way that exposes sensitive data to a large amount of risk.

COUNTRY VARIANCES

There are many issues that should be considered when deciding to engage in overseas outsourcing. A common misconception is that other countries are just like us, so you are dealing with a "mini United States." That is not the case. Your company's ability to enforce contractual obligations in a foreign country is not the same as it is here in the United States. Make certain to consult a lawyer specializing in laws as they relate to contracts for the particular country you plan on conducting business in.

There are production issues to consider as well. The power grids of most countries are not on par with those of either the United States or the United Kingdom. Having a reliable backup plan in the case of a power outage is critical. If there is network connectivity between you and the overseas company, there are other production issues to consider. Having sufficient bandwidth is one of the biggest challenges. A full T1 line provides 1.5 megabits of throughput. It may sound like a lot, but consider the networking experience if 60 overseas personnel were sharing the same T1 line. Imagine trying to work remotely over a modem line while sharing it with a couple of your co-workers. Attachments of any size are likely to cripple network responsiveness.

And how reliable is the Internet access, wide area network (WAN) switches, and other network hardware at the offshore site? How hard will it be to get production issues resolved for your overseas company? What would the impact be if your overseas vendor was knocked out of production for a day, a week, or even longer?

Even the local cultural norms need to be considered. A company with a high-pressure atmosphere might not interact well with a culture that is laid back. Since the salaries of overseas engineers are much less than those here in the United States, turnover is a big issue. It is not the engineer making $45 per hour chasing a job that pays $55 per hour. It is more like the $5.50 per hour engineer chasing the $6 per hour job. Once the effort is spent training them, they know that they are more marketable and will move from job to job for raises that would not tempt domestic workers.

Export restrictions also vary from country to country. Both the United States and the United Kingdom have restrictions on the technologies that can be exported to certain countries. The particular security appliance that your company uses or even the specific encryption algorithm may be forbidden from being exported to any number of countries. The U.S. Department of Commerce has information on such restrictions. Make sure you do your research prior to engaging in business with a company located in a foreign company. You could find yourself faced with the decision of either not conducting business that requires the use of tight security controls with a given country, or lessening those controls to meet the export restrictions. The Web site at www.bis.doc.gov/Encryption/ has more information.

In spite of all the warnings I've just given, the reality is that off-shoring is here to stay. Companies are not going to walk away from what is considered a nearly endless source of low-cost labor. From a pragmatic standpoint, I'm not suggesting a total moratorium on outsourcing, either. However, as with anything, the best decision is always a well-informed one. Many companies are taking unnecessary risks, and they don't save the kind of money that they had forecasted because they've failed to look at the big picture.

It is important to consider the logistical challenges, the political realities, the security implications, and the impact to your customer base if personal information is hacked at the facility of one of your overseas service providers. Off-shoring goes beyond just dollars and cents, and hence the decision to outsource should not be made solely by the CFO, but should include input from the CSO and the CTO as well.

POLITICAL REALITIES

I have heard it stated many times that people in this country are "U.S.-centric." To a certain point, I feel that is a good thing and can be attributed to a sense of patriotism and national pride. Well, citizens around the world are devoted to their home countries for the same reasons. And some of those countries may not particularly like the United States at any given time due to the political issues of the day. As of this writing, for example, the United States has military combat forces in both Iraq and Afghanistan. Many people in these nations are close to others in countries such as Iran and Syria, both of whom are not allies of the United States. Sending sensitive information to countries located in that region, such as India or Pakistan, therefore carries an added level of risk. What would the potential fallout be if the private financial or health information of your customers got hacked by a jihadist who got a job in one of those off-shore companies? One of the quickest ways to inflict pain on the United States is to hit the financial sector. Getting a job at a company located in that part of the world with an off-shore business relationship with a U.S.-based company would give them easy access to sensitive information, and potentially, an easy way to strike a blow.

A U.S. citizen caught stealing sensitive financial or health-care related information risks criminal charges, and being barred from holding such positions ever again. Does the same hold true in countries such as India and Pakistan? At best, their data privacy laws are weak compared to those in either the United States or the United Kingdom. Actual criminal enforcement of data privacy laws is almost non-existent. Compound that with the limitations of their background checks, and an individual could just move to a different part of the country and start with a clean slate. It would be as if I were convicted of embezzlement in Texas, but the conviction did not show up on a background check at the bank in New York where I just applied for a job. Due to these limitations, I recommend that companies think long and hard about what types of information they send off-shore. The hard reality is that you don't know what you don't know, and there's no good way to perform thorough background checks on employees in many of the countries that U.S. based corporations are doing business with.

OUTSOURCING SECURITY

In addition to the local cultural and political factors involved in out-sourcing, in many cases, by outsourcing you are entrusting responsibility for the security of your company's data. In part, this is because it simply is not possible to monitor a company located halfway around the world. This is not always a negative; just bear in mind that verifying controls are in place is complicated when the company is located on a different continent. Such a security arrangement is even worse if your foreign company is managing the firewall that separates your network from theirs at their facility. Are you sure that tight controls are in place, or has the effectiveness of the firewall just been eliminated? If the firewall is being blamed for a connectivity problem or a network throughput issue, will the off-shore engineers just permit any traffic to traverse them to "solve" the problem? Depending on the technical specifics of the implementation, you could be making the network of the foreign company a virtual extension of your own. The old adage that a chain is only as strong as its weakest link applies here. All the security measures that your company employs could be negated by the lack of security at the network of your outsourced service provider's enterprise.

Beyond the security issue of attack from would-be hackers, how certain are you that your company's information is not being co-mingled with data from other companies the vendor is working with? How sure are you that they won't sell your sensitive data to a competitor for the right price? Be careful about sending R&D data overseas. Identity theft is also a major issue, so take care in sending names and Social Security numbers overseas.

The best way to protect data is to keep the same standards no matter where the data is being held. For example, if it's sensitive enough to be encrypted in the United States, don't send it off-shore unless your vendors can encrypt it with an algorithm of similar strength. Also consider not sending sensitive data elements such as Social Security numbers off-shore. Use a Customer Identification Number instead. This would still allow the off-shore service provider to track the records as needed, while limiting your customers' exposure to the risk of identity theft.

PRODUCTION SUPPORT AND CALL CENTERS

I do not recommend using overseas personnel for production support on systems that either contain sensitive data or are mission critical. This is due to security as well as availability issues. For one thing, not all production support issues can be remedied remotely. Sometimes you need to have trained engineering personnel to physically touch a system in order to fix a production issue. It is common practice for support personnel to be given highly privileged access to the systems that they support. While this can be very helpful for resolving production problems, it also makes stealing any data on the system very easy as well. Do not give away highly privileged access to systems on your company's internal network to somebody working in an office located half a planet away.

The United States has one of the most robust critical infrastructures in the world. Most countries do not have an electrical grid, a transportation infrastructure, or a telecommunications network that is on par with what we have here in the United States. If you have outsourced the support of your business critical systems to a company with a less robust critical infrastructure, they may not be there when you need them the most.

Another common practice is for companies to send their technical support call centers overseas. Overwhelmingly, the public does not like dealing with support personnel in a foreign country when calling for technical support. Most people already have a certain level of frustration because they have a computer problem that they need help with. That is why they are calling technical support in the first place. Compound that with issues such as the quality of the phone line, and a strong accent, both of which have an impact on customer satisfaction. The cost of alienating your customers is something that must be factored in when considered sending call center support overseas.

RESPONSIBLE OVERSEAS OUTSOURCING

So, how can a company realize the cost savings of using overseas outsourcing? My first recommendation is software development. It doesn't require granting any access to your company's computer systems, nor do you have to send sensitive personal data overseas. This is not an apples-to-apples comparison, however. When calculating your costs, be sure to build in more development time and application rewrites. Problems arise due to differences in the skill sets of overseas programmers and domestic ones, as well as different interpretations of the application requirements. Since most communications with overseas personnel are either over the phone or by e-mail, there is a greater chance for a misunderstanding when communicating application requirements. Command and control is simply more difficult in an overseas situation, so the chances of errors are greater.

Once the software is ready to be reviewed, have the application securely transmitted to your company. This way it can be reviewed locally to ensure it meets both functionality and security requirements. You should never have the same engineers who write the software support it in production. This is also applies to software development domestically. Such a practice violates the principle of separation of duties and, again, allows developers to exploit flaws they wrote in the code to compromise a production system.

As with other off-shore projects, only send personal data that is absolutely necessary. Protect your customers wherever possible. This can be done by only sending partial account numbers, or by using a customer identifier that's specific to your company. You can also take steps such as only sending the last four digits of an account number, rather than the entire number itself. Such steps do take an extra level of effort but will lower the risk to your customers, which in turn lowers your company's risks.

So, we've come to the end of a journey. Along the way, I have covered a number of issues ranging from policy making to regulations to off-shoring and much more. An overarching theme that has run throughout the book is that the field of data security is very involved, and in many aspects can be highly complex. I hope that what I have written has provided useful information and been thought provoking. No single person has all the answers, not even a 20-year veteran like me. I can't stress enough the importance of seeking out professionals in their respective fields so that when it comes to making decisions that will have a serious impact on your company, you'll have the comfort of knowing you're making fully informed ones.

APPENDIX A

THE TRUSTED COMPUTER SYSTEM EVALUATION CRITERIA (TCSEC)

ORANGE BOOK

The Trusted Computer System Evaluation Criteria (TCSEC) standard specifies degrees of trust with increasing level of trust ratings. Each level builds upon the previous one by adding security features and assurance to the user that the features work as designed. The various TCSEC standards are considered by many in the IT security field as a benchmark for denoting increasingly stringent security system configurations. Adapted from the United States Department of Defense Web site, the degrees of trust within the Orange Book rating system are as follows:

D – Minimal Protection

Any system that does not comply to any other category, or has failed to receive a higher classification.

C – Discretionary Protection

Discretionary protection applies to Trusted Computer Bases, TCBs, with optional object (i.e. file, directory, devices, etc.) protection.

C1 – Discretionary Security Protection

1)   Discretionary Access Control, for example, Access Control Lists (ACLs), User/Group/World protection.

2)   Usually for users who are all on the same security level.

3)   Username and Password protection and secure authorizations database (ADB).

4) Protected operating system and system operations mode.

5) Periodic integrity checking of TCB.

6) Tested security mechanisms with no obvious bypasses.

7) Documentation for User Security.

8) Documentation for Systems Administration Security.

9) Documentation for Security Testing.

10) TCB design documentation.

11) Typically for users on the same security level.

C2 – Controlled Access Protection

As C1 plus:

1) Object protection can be on a single-user basis, e.g. through an ACL or Trustee database.

2) Authorization for access may only be assigned by authorized users.

3) Object reuse protection (i.e. to avoid reallocation of secure deleted objects).

4) Mandatory identification and authorization procedures for users, e.g. username/password.

5) Full auditing of security events (i.e. date/time, event, user, success/failure, terminal ID).

6) Protected system mode of operation.

7) Added protection for authorization and audit data.

8) Documentation as C1 plus information on examining audit information.

B – Mandatory Protection

Division B specifies that the TCB protection systems should be mandatory, not discretionary.

B1 – Labeled Security Protection

As C2 plus:

1) Mandatory security and access labeling of all objects, e.g. files, processes, devices, etc.

2) Label integrity checking (e.g. maintenance of sensitivity labels when data is exported).

3) Auditing of labeled objects.

4)   Mandatory access control for all operations.

5)   Ability to specify security level printed on human-readable output (e.g. printers).

6)   Ability to specify security level on any machine-readable output.

7)   Enhanced auditing.

8)   Enhanced protection of Operating System.

9)   Improved documentation.

B2 – Structured Protection

As B1 plus:

1)   Notification of security level changes affecting interactive users.

2)   Hierarchical device labels.

3)   Mandatory access over all objects and devices.

4)   Trusted path communications between user and system.

5)   Tracking down of covert storage channels.

6)   Tighter system operations mode into multilevel independent units.

7)   Covert channel analysis.

8)   Improved security testing.

9)   Formal models of trusted computing base, or TCB.

10)   Version, update and patch analysis and auditing.

B3 – Security Domains

As B2 plus:

1)   ACLs additionally based on groups and identifiers.

2)   Trusted path access and authentication.

3)   Automatic security analysis.

4)   TCB models more formal.

5)   Auditing of security auditing events.

6)   Trusted recovery after system down and relevant documentation.

7)   Zero design flaws in TCB, and minimum implementation flaws.

A - Verified Protection

Division A is the highest security division.

A1 - Verified Protection

As B3 plus:

1) Formal methods and proof of integrity of TCB.

A2 and above

Provision is made for security levels higher than A2, although these have not yet been formally defined.

Source: United States Department of Defense

APPENDIX B

RAINBOW SERIES

The National Institute for Standards and Technology (NIST) has developed a "Rainbow Series" of standards. Each color addresses a different area within information security. The table below provides a reference of all of the various documents and standards in the Rainbow Series. Many of these documents can be found here: http://csrc.ncsl.nist.gov/publications/secpubs/rainbow/index.html.

As with the Orange Book, all of the respective colored books in the Rainbow Series provide in-depth security information on the specific area as indicated in their title. They serve as an excellent reference for anybody having security issues in a given area.

NIST Rainbow Series

Document	Title	Date	Color
5200.28-STD	*DoD Trusted Computer Systems Evaluation Criteria*	15 Aug 1983	Orange Book
CSC-STD-002-85	*DoD Password Management Guideline*	12 Apr 1985	Green Book
CSC-STS-003-85	*Guidance for applying TCSEC in Specific Environments*	25 Jun 1985	Yellow Book
NCSC-TG-001	*A Guide to Understanding Audit in Trusted Systems*	1 Jun 1988	Tan Book
NCSC-TG-002	*Trusted Product Security Evaluation Program*	22 Jun 1990	Bright Blue Book
NCSC-TG-003	*Discretionary Access Control in Trusted Systems*	30 Sep 1987	Neon Orange Book

Document	Title	Date	Color
NCSC-TG-004	*Glossary of Computer Security Terms*	21 Oct 1988	Aqua Book
NCSC-TG-005	*Trusted Network Interpretation*	31 Jul 1987	Red Book
NCSC-TG-006	*Configuration Management in Trusted Systems*	28 Mar 1988	Amber Book
NCSC-TG-007	*A Guide to Understanding Design Documentation in Trusted Systems.*	6 Oct 1988	Burgundy Book
NCSC-TG-008	*A Guide to Understanding Trusted Distribution in Trusted Systems.*	15 Dec 1988	Dark Lavender Book
NCSC-TG-009	*Computer Security Subsystem Interpretation of the TCSEC.*	16 Sep 1988	Venice Blue Book
NCSC-TG-010	*A Guide to Understanding Security Modeling in Trusted Systems*	October 1992	Aqua Book
NCSC-TG-011	*Trusted Network Interpretation Environments Guideline (TNI)*	1 August 1990	Red Book
NCSC-TG-013 V2	*RAMP Program Document*	1 March 1995	Pink Book
NCSC-TG-014	*Guidelines for Formal Verification Systems.*	1 Apr 1989	Purple Book
NCSC-TG-015	*Guide to Understanding Trusted Facility Management.*	18 Oct 1989	Brown Book
NCSC-TG-016	*Guidelines for Writing Trusted Facility Manuals*	October 1992	Yellow-Green Book
NCSC-TG-017	*Identification and Authentication in Trusted Systems*	September 1991	Light Blue Book
NCSC-TG-018	*Object Reuse in Trusted Systems'*	July 1992	Light Blue Book
NCSC-TG-019	*Trusted Product Evaluation Questionnaire.*	2 May 1992	Blue Book

Document	Title	Date	Color
NCSC-TG-020	*Trusted UNIX Working Group (TRUSIX) Rationale for Selecting Access Control List Features for the UNIX® System*	7 July 1989	Silver Book
NCSC-TG-021	Trusted Database Management System Interpretation of the TCSEC (TDI)	April 1991	Purple Book
NCSC-TG-022	*Trusted Recovery in Trusted Systems*	30 December 1991	Yellow Book
NCSC-TG-023	Security Testing and Test Documentation in Trusted Systems		Bright Orange Book
NCSC-TG-024 Vol. 1/4	*Procurement of Trusted Systems: An Introduction to Procurement Initiators on Computer Security Requirements*	December 1992	Purple Book
NCSC-TG-024 Vol. 2/4	*Procurement of Trusted Systems: Language for RFP Specifications and Statements of Work*	30 June 1993	Purple Book
NCSC-TG-024 Vol. 3/4	*Procurement of Trusted Systems: Computer Security Contract Data Requirements List and Data Item Description*	28 February 1994	Purple Book
NCSC-TG-024 Vol. 4/4	*Procurement of Trusted Systems: How to Evaluate a Bidder's Proposal Document*	Publication TBA	Purple Book
NCSC-TG-025	*Guide to Understanding Data Remanence in Automated Information Systems.*	September 1991	Forest Green Book
NCSC-TG-026	Writing the Security Features User's Guide for Trusted Systems	September 1991	Hot Peach Book

Document	Title	Date	Color
NCSC-TG-027	Information System Security Officer Responsibilities for Automated Information Systems	May 1992	Turquoise Book
NCSC-TG-028	Assessing Controlled Access Protection	25 May 1992	Violet Book
NCSC-TG-029	*Certification and Accreditation Concepts*	January 1994	Blue Book

Source: National Institute of Standards and Technology—http://www.nist.gov/

APPENDIX C

THE INTERNATIONAL ORGANIZATION FOR STANDARDIZATION (ISO)

The International Organization for Standardization's (ISO's) main products are the International Standards, but the ISO also creates Technical Reports, Technical Specifications, Publicly Available Specifications, Technical Corrigenda, and Guides.

International Standards are numbered, and have a format that contains *ISO[/IEC][/ASTM] [IS] nnnnn[:yyyy] Title*, where *nnnnn* is the standard number, *yyyy* is the year published, and *Title* describes the subject. *IEC* will only be included in instances where the standard results from the work of JTC1 (the "Joint Technical Committee"; see below). *ASTM* is included in cases where the standards were developed in cooperation with ASTM International. The date and *IS* will always be left off in instances of either incomplete or unpublished standards.

- **Technical Reports** are issued in instances where a technical committee has collected data of a different kind from that which is normally published as an International Standard.
- **Technical Specifications** are produced in those instances when the subject in question is still under development.
- **Publicly Available Specifications** may be "an intermediate specification, published prior to the development of a full International Standard, or, in IEC may be a 'dual logo' publication published in collaboration with an external organization." Both are named by convention similar to Technical Reports, for example:
- ISO/TS 16952-1:2006 Technical product documentation—Reference designation system—Part 1: General application rules
- ISO/PAS 11154:2006 Road vehicles—Roof load carriers

ISO will on rare occasions issue a Technical Corrigendum. These are amendments to existing standards because of minor technical flaws, improvements to usability, or to extend applicability in a limited way. Generally, these are issued with the expectation that the affected standard will be updated or withdrawn at its next scheduled review.

ISO Guides are meta-standards covering "matters related to international standardization," They are named in the format *ISO[/IEC] Guide N:yyyy: Title*, for example:

- ISO/IEC Guide 2:2004 Standardization and related activities—General vocabulary
- ISO/IEC Guide 65:1996 General requirements for bodies operating product certification systems

ISO/IEC Joint Technical Committee 1

To deal with the consequences of substantial overlap in areas of standardization and work related to information technology, ISO and IEC formed a Joint Technical Committee known as the ISO/IEC JTC1. It was the first such committee, and to date remains the only one.

Its official mandate is to develop, maintain, promote, and facilitate IT standards required by global markets meeting business and user requirements concerning:

- the design and development of IT systems and tools,
- the performance and quality of IT products and systems,
- the security of IT systems and information,
- the portability of application programs,
- the interoperability of IT products and systems,
- the unified tools and environments,
- the harmonized IT vocabulary, and
- the user-friendly and ergonomically-designed user interfaces.

There are currently 18 sub-committees:

- SC 02 – Coded Character Sets
- SC 06 – Telecommunications and Information Exchange Between Systems
- SC 07 – Software and System Engineering
- TC 46/SC 9 – Information and Documentation – Identification and Description
- SC 17 – Cards and Personal Identification
- SC 22 – Programming Languages, their Environments and Systems Software Interfaces
- SC 23 – Removable Digital Storage Media Utilizing Optical and/or Magnetic Recording

- SC 24 – Computer Graphics and Image Processing
- SC 25 – Interconnection of Information Technology Equipment
- SC 27 – IT Security Techniques
- SC 28 – Office Equipment
- SC 29 – Coding of Audio, Picture, and Multimedia and Hypermedia Information
- SC 31 – Automatic Identification and Data Capture Techniques
- SC 32 – Data Management and Interchange
- SC 34 – Document Description and Processing Languages
- SC 35 – User Interfaces
- SC 36 – Information Technology for Learning, Education, and Training
- SC 37 – Biometrics

Membership in ISO/IEC JTC1 is restricted in much the same way as membership in either of the two parent organizations. A member can be either participating (p) or observing (O), and the difference is mainly the ability to vote on proposed standards and other products. There is no requirement for any member to maintain either (or any) status on all of the sub-committees. Although rare, sub-committees can be created to deal with new situations (SC 37 was approved in 2002) or disbanded if the area of work is no longer relevant.

There are 157 national members, out of the 198 total countries in the world. ISO has three membership categories:

- *Member bodies* are national bodies that are considered to be the most representative standards body in each country. These are the only members of ISO that have voting rights.
- *Correspondent members* are countries that do not have a standards organization of their own. These members are informed about the work going on in ISO but are not allowed to take part in the actual standardization work.
- *Subscriber members* are countries with small economies. These have reduced membership fees but can follow the development of new standards.

Countries and their Membership status in the International Organization for Standardization (ISO):

ISO Members by Country

Country A2 Code	Country A3 Code	Country Code No.	Country Name (English)	Standards Body	ISO Status
AF	AFG	004	Afghanistan	ANSA	Correspondent Member
AL	ALB	008	Albania	DPS	Correspondent Member

Country A2 Code	Country A3 Code	Country Code No.	Country Name (English)	Standards Body	ISO Status
DZ	DZA	012	Algeria	IANOR	Member Body
AD	AND	020	Andorra	IRAM	Member Body
AO	AGO	024	Angola	IANORQ	Correspondent Member
AG	ATG	028	Antigua & Barbuda	ABBS	Subscriber Member
AR	ARG	032	Argentina	IRAM	Member Body
AM	ARM	051	Armenia	SARM	Member Body
AU	AUS	036	Australia	SA	Member Body
AT	AUT	040	Austria	ON	Member Body
AZ	AZE	031	Azerbaijan	AZSTAND	Member Body
BS	BHS	044	Bahamas	-	
BH	BHR	048	Bahrain	BMSD	Member Body
BD	BGD	050	Bangladesh	BSTI	Member Body
BB	BRB	052	Barbados	BNSI	Member Body
BY	BLR	112	Belarus	BELST	Member Body
BE	BEL	056	Belgium	NBN	Member Body
BZ	BLZ	084	Belize	-	
BJ	BEN	204	Benin	CEBENOR	Correspondent Member
BT	BTN	064	Bhutan	SQCA	Correspondent Member
BO	BOL	068	Bolivia	IBNORCA	Correspondent Member
BA	BIH	070	Bosnia & Herzegovina	BASMP	Member Body
BW	BWA	072	Botswana	BOBS	Member Body
BR	BRA	076	Brazil	ABNT	Member Body
BN	BRB	096	Brunei Darussalam	CPRU	Correspondent Member
BG	BGR	100	Bulgaria	BDS	Member Body
BF	BFA	854	Burkina Faso	FASONORM	Correspondent Member

Country A2 Code	Country A3 Code	Country Code No.	Country Name (English)	Standards Body	ISO Status
MM (BU)	MMR	104	Myanmar (Burma)	-	
BI	BDI	108	Burundi	BBN	Subscriber Member
KH	KHM	116	Cambodia	ISC	Subscriber Member
CM	CMR	120	Cameroon	CDNQ	Correspondent Member
CA	CAN	124	Canada	SCC	Member Body
CV	CPV	132	Cape Verde	-	
CF	CAF	140	Central African Republic	-	
TD	TCD	148	Chad	-	
CL	CHL	52	Chile	INN	Member Body
CN	CHN	156	China	SAC	Member Body
CO	COL	170	Colombia	ICONTEC	Member Body
KM	COM	174	Comoros	-	
CG	COG	178	Congo, Republic of the	-	
CD (ZR)	COD	180	Congo, Democratic Republic of the (Zaire)	OCC	Member Body
CR	CRI	188	Costa Rica	INTECO	Member Body
CI	CIV	384	Côte d'Ivoire	CODINORM	Member Body
HR	HRV	191	Croatia	HZN	Member Body
CU	CUB	192	Cuba	NC	Member Body
CY	CYP	196	Cyprus	CYS	Member Body
CZ	CZE	203	Czech Republic	CNI	Member Body
DK	DNK	208	Denmark	DS	Member Body
DJ	DJI	262	Djibouti	-	
DM	DMA	212	Dominica	DBOS	Subscriber Member

Country A2 Code	Country A3 Code	Country Code No.	Country Name (English)	Standards Body	ISO Status
DO	DOM	214	Dominican Republic	DIGINOR	Correspondent Member
EC	ECU	218	Ecuador	INEN	Member Body
EG	EGY	818	Egypt	EOS	Member Body
SV	SLV	222	El Salvador	CONACYT	Correspondent Member
GQ	GNQ	226	Equatorial Guinea	-	
ER	ERI	232	Eritrea	ESI	Correspondent Member
EE	EST	233	Estonia	EVS	Correspondent Member
ET	ETH	231	Ethiopia	QSAE	Member Body
FJ	FJI	242	Fiji	FTSQCO	Member Body
FI	FIN	246	Finland	SFS	Member Body
FR	FRA	250	France	AFNOR	Member Body
GA	GAB	266	Gabon	-	
GM	GMB	270	Gambia, The	-	
GE	GEO	268	Georgia	GEOSTM	Correspondent Member
DE	DEU	276	Germany	DIN	Member Body
GH	GHA	288	Ghana	GSB	Member Body
GR	GRC	300	Greece	ELOT	Member Body
GD	GRD	308	Grenada	-	
GT	GTM	320	Guatemala	COGUANOR	Correspondent Member
GN	GIN	324	Guinea	INNM	Correspondent Member
GW	GNB	624	Guinea-Bissau	DSNPQ	Correspondent Member
GY	GUY	328	Guyana	GNBS	Subscriber Member
HT	HTI	332	Haiti	-	

Country A2 Code	Country A3 Code	Country Code No.	Country Name (English)	Standards Body	ISO Status
HN	HND	340	Honduras	COHCIT	Subscriber Member
HK	HKG	344	Hong Kong, China	ITCHKSAR	Correspondent Member
HU	HUN	348	Hungary	MSZT	Member Body
IS	ISL	352	Iceland	IST	Member Body
IN	IND	356	India	BIS	Member Body
ID	IDN	360	Indonesia	BSN	Member Body
IR	IRN	364	Iran, Islamic Republic of	ISIRTI	Member Body
IQ	IRW	368	Iraq	COSQC	Member Body
IE	IRL	372	Ireland	NSAI	Member Body
IL	ISR	376	Israel	SII	Member Body
IT	ITA	380	Italy	UNI	Member Body
JM	JAM	388	Jamaica	JBS	Member Body
JP	JPN	392	Japan	JISC	Member Body
JO	JOR	400	Jordan	JISM	Member Body
KZ	KAZ	398	Kazakhstan	KAZMEMST	Member Body
KE	KEN	404	Kenya	KEBS	Member Body
KI	KIR	296	Kiribati	-	
KP	PRK	408	Korea, Democratic People's Republic	CSK	Member Body
KR	KOR	410	Korea, Republic of	KATS	Member Body
KW	KWT	414	Kuwait	KOWSMD	Member Body
KG	KGZ	417	Kyrgyzstan	KYRGYZST	Correspondent Member
LA	LAO	418	Laos (Lao People's Democratic Republic)	DISM	Subscriber Member

Country A2 Code	Country A3 Code	Country Code No.	Country Name (English)	Standards Body	ISO Status
LV	LVA	428	Latvia	LVS	Correspondent Member
LB	LBN	422	Lebanon	LIBNOR	Member Body
LS	LSO	426	Lesotho	LSQAS	Subscriber Member
LR	LBR	430	Liberia	-	
LY	LBY	434	Libyan Arab Jamahiriya	LNCSM	Member Body
LI	LIE	438	Liechtenstein	-	
LT	LTU	440	Lithuania	LST	Correspondent Member
LU	LUX	442	Luxembourg	SEE	Member Body
MO	MAC	446	Macau (Macau China)	CPTTM	Correspondent Member
MK	MKD	807	Macedonia, The former Yugoslav Republic of	ISRM	Member Body
MG	MDG	450	Madagascar	BNM	Correspondent Member
MW	MWI	454	Malawi	MBS	Correspondent Member
MY	MYS	458	Malaysia	DSM	Member Body
MV	MDV	462	Maldives	-	
ML	MLI	466	Mali	MLIDNI	Correspondent Member
MT	MLT	470	Malta	MSA	Member Body
MH	MHL	584	Marshall Islands	-	
MR	MRT	478	Mauritania	-	
MU	MUS	480	Mauritius	MSB	Member Body
MX	MEX	484	Mexico	DGN	Member Body

Country A2 Code	Country A3 Code	Country Code No.	Country Name (English)	Standards Body	ISO Status
FM	FSM	583	Micronesia, Federated States Of	-	
MD	MDA	498	Moldova, Republic of	MOLDST	Correspondent Member
MC	MCO	492	Monaco	-	
MN	MNG	496	Mongolia	MASM	Member Body
(YS)[2]	-	-	Montenegro	-	
MA	MAR	504	Morocco	SNIMA	Member Body
MZ	MOZ	508	Mozambique	INNOQ	Correspondent Member
MM	MMR	104	Myanmar	MSTRD	Correspondent Member
NA	NAM	516	Namibia	NSIQO	Correspondent Member
NR	NRU	520	Nauru	-	
NP	NPL	524	Nepal	NBSM	Correspondent Member
NL	NLD	528	The Netherlands	NEN	Member Body
NZ	NZL	554	New Zealand	SNZ	Member Body
NI	NIC	558	Nicaragua	DTNM	Correspondent Member
NE	NER	562	Niger	DNQM	Correspondent Member
NG	NGA	566	Nigeria	SON	Member Body
NO	NOR	578	Norway	SN	Member Body
OM	OMN	512	Oman	DGSM	Member Body
PK	PAK	586	Pakistan	PSQCA	Member Body
PW	PLW	585	Palau	-	
PS	PSE	275	Palestinian State[3]	PSI	Correspondent Member
PA	PAN	591	Panama	COPANIT	Member Body

Country A2 Code	Country A3 Code	Country Code No.	Country Name (English)	Standards Body	ISO Status
PG	PNG	598	Papua New Guinea	NISIT	Correspondent Member
PY	PRY	600	Paraguay	INTN	Correspondent Member
PE	PER	604	Peru	INDECOPI	Member Body
PH	PHL	608	The Philippines	BPS	Member Body
PL	POL	616	Poland	PKN	Member Body
PT	PRT	620	Portugal	IPQ	Member Body
QA	QAT	634	Qatar	QS	Member Body
RO	ROU	642	Romania	ASRO	Member Body
RU	RUS	643	Russian Federation	GOST R	Member Body
RW	RWA	646	Rwanda	RBS	Correspondent Member
KN	KNA	659	St. Kitts & Nevis	-	
LC	LCA	662	St. Lucia	SLBS	Member Body
VC	VCT	670	Saint Vincent and the Grenadines	SVGBS	Subscriber Member
WS	WSM	882	Samoa	-	
SM	SMR	674	San Marino	-	
ST	STP	678	São Tomé & Príncipe	-	
SA	SAU	682	Saudi Arabia	SASO	Member Body
SN	SEN	686	Senegal	ASN	Correspondent Member
CS	SCG	891	Serbia	ISS	Member Body
SC	SYC	690	Seychelles	SBS	Correspondent Member
SL	SLE	694	Sierra Leone	-	
SG	SGP	702	Singapore	SPRING SG	Member Body
SK	SVK	703	Slovakia	SUTN	Member Body

Country A2 Code	Country A3 Code	Country Code No.	Country Name (English)	Standards Body	ISO Status
SI	SVN	705	Slovenia	SIST	Member Body
SB	SLB	090	Solomon Islands	-	
SO	SOM	706	Somalia	-	
ZA	ZAF	710	South Africa	SABS	Member Body
ES	ESP	724	Spain	AENOR	Member Body
LK	LKA	144	Sri Lanka	SLSI	Member Body
SD	SDN	736	Sudan	SSMO	Member Body
SR	SUR	740	Suriname	-	
SZ	SWZ	748	Swaziland	SQAS	Correspondent Member
SE	SWE	752	Sweden	SIS	Member Body
CH	CHE	756	Switzerland	SNV	Member Body
SY	SYR	760	Syrian Arab Republic	SASMO	Member Body
TW	TWN	158	Taiwan (Province of China)	-	
TJ	TJK	762	Tajikistan	TJKSTN	Correspondent Member
TZ	TZA	834	Tanzania, United Republic of	TBS	Member Body
TH	THA	764	Thailand	TISI	Member Body
TL(TP)	TLS	206	Timor Leste, Democratic Republic of (East Timor)	-	
TG	TGO	768	Togo	CSN	Correspondent Member
TO	TON	776	Tonga	-	
TT	TTO	780	Trinidad & Tobago	TTBS	Member Body
TN	TUN	788	Tunisia	INNORPI	Member Body

Country A2 Code	Country A3 Code	Country Code No.	Country Name (English)	Standards Body	ISO Status
TR	TUR	792	Turkey	TSE	Member Body
TM	TKM	795	Turkmenistan	MSST	Correspondent Member
TV	TUV	798	Tuvalu	-	
UG	UGA	800	Uganda	UNBS	Correspondent Member
UA	UKR	804	Ukraine	DSSU	Member Body
AE	ARE	784	United Arab Emirates	ESMA	Member Body
GB	GBR	826	United Kingdom (Great Britain)	BSI	Member Body
US	USA	840	United States	ANSI	Member Body
UY	URY	858	Uruguay	UNIT	Member Body
UZ	UZB	860	Uzbekistan	UZSTANDARD	Member Body
VU	VUT	548	Vanuatu	-	
VA	VAT	336	Vatican City (Holy See)	-	
VE	VEN	862	Venezuela	FONDONORMA	Member Body
VN	VNM	704	Vietnam	TCVN	Member Body
EH	ESH	732	Western Sahara	-	
YE	YEM	887	Yemen	YSMO	Correspondent Member
ZM	ZMB	894	Zambia	ZABS	Correspondent Member
ZW	ZWE	816	Zimbabwe	SAZ	Member Body

Source: The International Organization for Standardization—www.iso.org

GLOSSARY

Access Control List: An ACL is a list of users or groups that are allowed access to a specific system resource. When a router is sent a new route, it adds that information to its ACL list, making it iterative in nature. The more complete the ACL, the more efficient it is.

Administrator Account: A type of user account on a computer generally reserved to support personnel chartered with maintaining the system. On Windows-based servers, an administrator account is capable of performing any task.

Adware: Software that has an advertising function integrated into it. Usually associated with software that is given away for free, but seeks voluntary donations from users. Generally used by programmers as a way to recover some of the costs of developing the program in the first place.

Analog or *analogue:* Any variable signal continuous in both time and amplitude. This differs from digital signals, which are either on or off. In the context of network data transmissions, analog is generally associated with using modems. Analog is also susceptible to interference from outside noise. Similar to the way you can have a "bad" connection with telephone conservations, analog network data transmissions can suffer from background noise as well.

Anonymous FTP: Anonymous FTP does not require either a username or a password. It is considered a security risk due to the lack of authentication requirements.

Asymmetric Cryptography: A form of encryption consisting of a public and private key pair. The private key is kept secret, while the public key can be sent out. Much slower than symmetric cryptography, it is generally only used to encrypt smaller amounts of data.

Authentication: The act of verifying the identity of an end-user or a system. It is usually the first half of the overall process users go through when trying to gain access to a system or data. The second half is authorization.

Authorization: Once a user's identity has been verified (authentication), the authorization process determines if they have permission to access the system or data they are attempting to reach.

Bastion Host: A bastion host is a server that has been configured to very strict security standards. This is generally due to the nature of the role it is fulfilling, or where on the network it is located. A bastion host server may be in a part of the network that is considered either semi-trusted or event un-trusted. A part of the network accessible by either the public or other companies, a bastion host server may also be used to protect other parts of the network. For example, it can serve as a firewall.

Block Cipher: A method in cryptography that can take messages of variable size and encrypt them into blocks of a fixed length, typically 64, 128, or 256 bits in length.

Bluejacking: The act of sending unwanted messages to a Bluetooth device, such as a cell phone or a PDA. It can also include unsolicited messages akin to junk mail.

Bluesnarfing: The act of obtaining unauthorized access to information being transmitted between two Bluetooth-enabled devices such as cell phones or PDAs. The data can include contact lists, calendars, and even e-mails and text messages. A defense against Bluesnarfing is to set your device to "hidden" rather than "discoverable."

Bluetooth: An industry standard for short-range wireless networks, also known as personal area networks. Bluetooth technology is commonly used with mobile phones, laptops, printers, digital cameras, and more.

Bollard: Originally associated generally with shipping docks, a bollard is a short vertical post. Today they are also used to direct traffic and to provide protection at building entrances.

British Standards Institute (BSI): A division of the BSI group, it sets many of the data security standards in the United Kingdom. The ISO 17799, which is widely used in the United States, is derived from the BS 7799.

Brute-Force Attack: A type of attack that uses a trial-and-error method to find legitimate authentication credentials. The attack is generally designed to find out the password of a legitimate user.

Business Continuity Planning (BCP): The practice of creating a plan enabling a company to properly respond to a loss of assets from either an act of God or man. A BCP plan will include planning, documenting, re-documenting, and testing. They are generally customized to meet the specific needs of a given organization as well as where a company is located. For example, a company based in Florida will need to prepare for a hurricane more than it would an earthquake.

Client/Server Applications: A type of application architecture consisting of two parts, a client component and a server component. The server resides on a network-shared resource. The client side generally resides on an end-user's workstation or laptop. E-mail is a good example, with a program such as Outlook being the client portion and MS Exchange being the server portion.

Cold Site: A disaster-recovery facility that provides only the physical space for recovery operations. The organization using the space is responsible for providing its own hardware and software systems.

Common Criteria: An international standard for computer security. Common criteria provides a framework in which organizations can specify their security requirements to their vendors and suppliers. It is designed to help provide assurances that certain specifications related to system configuration and security have in fact been met.

Cookies: Small pieces of data sent to your computer generally from an Internet site to help the site track that you've been there. Sometimes also referred to as a tracking cookie.

Daemon: In UNIX and Linux environments, a daemon is a program that runs in the background, usually initiated as an automated process requiring no direct manual intervention.

Degaussing: A process for irretrievably removing data from a hard drive or other magnetic storage media. Deemed far more secure than merely using a delete function native to most operating systems and applications.

Demilitarized Zone: In the context of computer networking, a Demilitarized Zone (DMZ) denotes a segment of a network that is at a higher risk of attack. Generally placed near the outside perimeter of a company's computer network. Since computers within a DMZ are more susceptible to attack, they need to be configured to stricter security guidelines. It is also very common to have a firewall protecting the interior zone of a company's network from the DMZ.

Denial-of-Service Attack (DoS attack): A type of electronic attack designed to either greatly degrade a system or to cause it to crash altogether.

Development Environment: The part of a network in which ongoing software development occurs. The greater the separation between production systems and development systems the better. Since the development process consists of trial and error, a lack of appropriate separation could cause system outages in a production environment.

Dictionary Attack: A hacking technique that uses words found in a dictionary to guess passwords and pass phrases in order to gain unauthorized system access. Can be defeated, or at least slowed, by two-factor authentication or longer, more complex passwords.

Digital: Data transmissions that are either "on" or "off." Analog transmissions, on the other hand, are continuous at various frequencies. Most current-day data transmission lines in the United States use digital rather than analog.

Dynamic Host Configuration Protocol (DHCP): A technique for temporarily "leasing" IP addresses to computers. Generally, DHCP leased addresses are given to end-user systems such as workstations or laptops, while servers and other shared network resources have permanently assigned TCP/IP addresses. At the end of a lease period, a new IP address would be assigned. The main strength of DHCP is that it saves time, because you don't have to manually assign individuals IP addresses to each new workstation or laptop that is added to the network.

Encrypted Transport Protocol: A term given to transport protocols that encrypt the data payload as they move the data from one system to another. Examples include SSH, IPSec, and SSL.

Encryption: The mathematical process of alternating data and changing it into cipher text. Decryption is the reverse process. Encryption has been used for thousands of years to exchange data while protecting its confidentiality.

Exploits: Weaknesses discovered in software such as operating systems and applications that a hacker can leverage to gain unauthorized access, steal data, or cause system interruptions.

Extranet: A process to connect a portion of a computer network of two separate organizations. Generally considered more secure than the Internet, extranets use dedicated communication lines to connect the two companies.

Firecall ID: A one-time-use account/password combination generally used for remote support of computer systems by engineering personnel. Firecall IDs are considered nearly unbreakable because they are not re-used.

Firewall: A security device that is designed to permit only specifically allowed data communications to enter or exit a computer network. Those not specifically allowed are generally blocked. Firewalls may be either hardware or software based. Software-based firewalls are generally installed on end-user systems to provide a level of protection. Hardware firewalls are generally deployed to protect different areas of a computer network at its outward perimeter.

Firewall Rules: Rules that specify which communication will be allowed to traverse a firewall. Ideally, firewall rules should be written as specifically as possible. If mis-configured, or if overly broad rules are entered, the firewall's effectiveness as a security device will be diminished.

FTP: File Transport Protocol. FTP is a transport protocol used to transmit data. FTP transmits data in clear text, so it is not considered a secure protocol. FTP is also considered an interactive protocol as it allows users to perform certain functions at the remote system.

FTPS: A secure form of the FTP protocol incorporating Secure Sockets Layer (SSL) encryption.

Gigabyte: A unit of information or computer storage equal to one billion bytes. It is commonly abbreviated GB and is the equivalent of 1,000 megabytes.

Graphical User Interface (GUI): A pictorial interface generally in the form of an icon, making many operations as easy as point and click. For example, printing a document is as easy as clicking on a icon that looks like a printer.

Hacking, Hacker: Hacking is the act of attempting to perform illegal, unauthorized, or unsolicited actions to computer systems. These acts can include the theft of data, defacing a web site, or interrupting with the normal operations of a computer. A person engaged in hacking is called a hacker.

Hashing: Sometimes referred to as a non-reversible form of encryption. A hash can take data of varying length and produce hash values of fixed length.

Hot Fix: A single software fix, or at times an accumulation of software fixes, used to resolve identified issues (bugs). Hot fixes may also be sent out quickly in response to a newly discovered vulnerability.

Hot Site: A backup site that allows an organization to resume business operations immediately in the event of a disaster. It includes all the needed infrastructure, space, and equipment.

HTTP: Hyper-Text Transport Protocol. The main communications protocol for transmitting data over the Internet. HTTP is considered insecure because it transmits data in the clear.

HTTPS: Hyper-Text Transport Protocol Secure. A secured form of the HTTP protocol that does encrypt data while in transit.

Hub: A device for connecting multiple instances of physical wiring, such as a twisted pair of fiber optics, together.

ID/fob: Generally a physical device known as a "token" that generates a number every 60 seconds and is used for authentication. Software ID/fobs are becoming more popular in recent years for use in cell phones and PDAs and are also less expensive then physical tokens.

Internet Protocol (IP): The foundation for a suite of protocols that is the de facto standard for transmitting data over the Internet. IP-based communication protocols are also used in the majority of computer networks around the world to transmit data.

Intrusion Detection Sensor (IDS): A device designed to detect and even prevent malicious events (hacking). IDS can be host-based and loaded directly onto servers, or network-based, to deter malicious data while in transit. Sensors can also be signature or anomaly based. Signature-based IDS sensors detect known attacks, while anomaly-based sensors look for unusually patterns as an indicator of malicious activity.

Intrusion Prevention Sensor (IPS): While considered an extension of IDS, IPS is more related to a firewall. IPS sensors attempt to make decisions on whether data transmissions are valid or not by actually inspecting the data while in transit.

IP Spoofing: Using an IP address to send data that does not belong to the actual source computer system. This is usually done to either conceal the true identity of the source computer or to impersonate a legitimate computer to gain unauthorized access into a network.

JPEG: A file extension denoting a picture file.

Kerberos: A system for allowing individuals to provide their identification securely over an otherwise insecure network. Once identified, a Kerberos ticket is issued, allowing end-users to access systems they are authorized to.

Listening Ports: Ports—openings for data connections on a computer—that "listen" for data in order to accept it. Many well-known communications protocols used pre-identified ports. For example, SSH uses port 22. A common security hole in many computers occurs when unused listening ports are left open. Unused ports should be closed.

MAC Address: An address that is burned onto most network adapter cards. A MAC address can act as a unique addressing identifier for computers on a network.

Maintenance Hooks: Sometimes also referred to as a back door, a maintenance hook allows a developer to gain access back into their programs by bypassing any security measures that may have been added after they've written the program. While effective for troubleshooting in a development environment, maintenance hooks represent a serious security hole in production systems.

Malware: A generic term given to software that is specially designed to perform either harmful or unauthorized acts to computer systems. Specific types of malware include viruses, Trojans, spyware, and worms.

Master Image File: A preconfigured image—including the operating system and all necessary programs—that is stored on a network-accessible computer. As new systems are brought into the network, a master image can merely be loaded onto it. This is much quicker and also lends itself to more consistency. In order for master image files to be most effective, they need to have patches, anti-virus files, and any other updates applied to them, as with any other computer system.

Megabit: A unit of measure that is most commonly used when referring to data transmission rates. Ethernet speeds, for example, can be set at 10, 100, or 1000 Mb/second.

Megabyte: Commonly abbreviated as MB, it is a unit of information or computer storage equal to 1024^2 bytes.

MS-DOS (MicroSoft Disk Operating System): An operating system that was made famous by Microsoft. It was commonly used by personal computers, except Apples, during the early years of the PC (1980s). DOS was gradually replaced by the more sophisticated operating systems of the day, such as Windows 3.1 and Windows 95.

Multipurpose Internet Mail Extensions (MIME): The de facto standard or format used for the vast majority of Internet e-mail. Since most e-mail is transmitted using the Simple Mail Transfer Protocol (SMTP), the two are often linked together and commonly referred to as SMTP/MIME e-mail.

Network Address Translation (NAT): A technique of changing the source IP address of a computer when it traverses a firewall. NAT hides the true IP address of internal systems that must communicate with servers on an outside network, making it a security measure. In a data transmission leaving a network, the source IP address would be changed through NAT to what is known as a virtual IP address actually belonging to the firewall. This way, the computer on the outside network never sees the true IP address of the internal system.

Patch: Software designed to fix problems with a program. A patch is often used to fix a security hole, but it can also improve usability in one way or another.

Ping: A networking tool used to determine whether a system is reachable on an IP-based network. A ping request will respond back that the system is reachable, along with how long it took to reach the remote host, or state that the remote host was unreachable.

Pretty Good Privacy (PGP): An encryption solution that is mainly used to protect e-mails. A weakness of PGP is the fact that it uses a more distributed form of certificate authentication than entities such as VeriSign. Whereas Verisign maintains centralized control over issuing and revoking digital certificates, PGP authentication is more distributed. Any company with a PGP server can issue digital certificates. This decentralization increases the risk of fraudulent digital signatures floating around.

Production System: A server that is used to either store production data or to fulfill a function in a production environment.

Protocol: Also known as a transport protocol, a protocol is a standard by which computers communicate with each other.

Proxy-based Firewall: A firewall that does not send out IP packets from the original host. It hides the identities of the internal hosts by using IP addresses assigned to the firewall itself. The integrity of the data in the message itself is maintained.

Removable Media Encryption (RME): A software solution that can encrypt data on removable storage devices such as floppy disks, CDs, thumb drives, PDAs, and more. Once attached to a computer that has removable media encryption installed on it, the host system will push the encryption onto the removable device. Any data loaded on the removable device will be encrypted at the hard drive level. This protects the confidentiality of the data if the device is stolen.

Root: In both Unix and Linux based operating systems, root is the name of the built-in account that has the highest level of privilege. Akin to "Administrator" on Windows-based computers, root can perform nearly any function on Unix or Linux based systems. Due care should be taken when giving individuals root-level privileges due to the powerful nature of the account.

Router: A device used for network. addressing. As data transmissions come to a router, it will determine the next path it should take from there. While not a firewall, a router can also block network communications.

Sally Port: A small controlled space with two doors. Essentially, one must enter the space and close the first door before opening the second to proceed. It is therefore akin to an airlock.

Secret-Key Cryptography: A form of cryptography in which the same secret key is used to both encrypt and decrypt. Also known as symmetric cryptography.

Service Pack: An accumulation of patches and fixes rolled up into a single large software update.

SFTP: Another secured variation of the FTP protocol. Where FTPS uses SSL to encrypt FTP traffic, SFTP uses the SSH protocol to provide the data confidentiality.

Shareware: A "try it before you buy it" type of software with a limited free trial period. A fee is usually required to obtain a user license for long-term use.

S/MIME: Provides encryption, authentication, and non-repudiation of data sent electronically, usually via e-mail.

Simple Mail Transfer Protocol (SMTP): The primary standard used for transmitting e-mails across the Internet.

Spyware: As the name suggests, spyware is software whose primary purpose is to gather information about the system that it resides on, or the data files contained therein, without the knowledge of the user. An example of spyware is a keystroke logger that can record every keystroke a user makes. This can be used to gain access to a user's account name and password.

Secure Socket Shell (SSH): SSH is a network transport protocol that establishes an encrypted channel between two computers. In addition to its encryption capabilities, SSH has other functions as well. SSH is an interactive protocol, allowing a user to take a certain amount of control of a remote system. Secure shell also has port forwarding, which is the capability of tunneling any transport protocol through it.

Secure Sockets Layer (SSL): SSL is the de facto protocol used to transmit data securely over the Internet. Web sites that are utilizing SSL can be identified by the fact the notation of HTTPS versus merely HTTP. The "S" at the end signifies that SSL is being utilized. It is important to note that SSL encrypts data while in transit between computers, and not while at rest on a computer.

Stateful Inspection Firewall: When computers transmit data between each other, the first thing that they do is establish an open channel of communication. This is also known as creating an open state. A stateful inspection firewall checks the state of those communication channels to make sure they are properly established. A common hacker trick is to transmit malformed transmission packets for illicit purposes.

Switch: A switch (or network switch) is a device that connects different network segments. Instead of using a computer's IP address, switches forward data based on their MAC address. A MAC address is the address burned onto a computer's network address card. A switch can be set to 10, 100, or even 1000 megabits per second, as well as full duplex or half duplex. Half duplex means a switch can only send or receive at any given time, whereas with full duplex it can do both simultaneously.

T1: Denotes the size of a transmission circuit, that has a capacity of 1.5 mbits/second of throughput.

TCP/IP: A suite of transport protocols used on a majority of computer networks today. TCP/IP is the de facto transport protocol used to transmit data over the Internet. IP stands for Internet Protocol, and TCP stands for Transmission Control Protocol. TCP has an error-checking functionality. Sometimes called a connection-oriented protocol, TCP performs checks to make sure that the data actually reaches its destination.

Trusted Computer System Evaluation Criteria (TCSEC): Created by the United Stated Department of Defense, TCSEC is a set of requirements that were established to assess the effectiveness of the security controls built into a computer system. Also known as the Orange Book, it is part of the Department of Defense's Rainbow Series.

Terabyte: A term used to denote data storage capacity. A terabyte is the equivalent of 1,000 gigabytes.

TLS: Created by Microsoft, Transport Lay Security is the predecessor of SSL. Like SSL, TLS is also used to securely transmit data over the Internet. There are slight differences between SSL and TLS, but the most recent versions of the two are TLS 1.0 and SSL 3.0.

Traceroute: A networking tool that can be used to determine the route taken by data as it traverses an IP-based network. In addition to showing the end-point, Traceroute will show every stop, more commonly referred to as hops, from the point of origin to the ultimate destination. Tracepath is the Linux version of Traceroute, which is primarily used on both Unix and Windows based systems.

Trojan Horse: As the mythical name suggests, a Trojan horse is a destructive program disguised as a legitimate piece of software. A Trojan horse may appear as a useful program, or as something of interest such as a sound file or an image file. At a high level, there are generally two types of Trojan horses. One is a legitimate piece of software that a hacker has corrupted. The other type is a program that a hacker has written himself, like an image file. Just like its ancient Greek counterpart, a computer Trojan horse needs to gain entrance to your computer system in order to function and is dependent on actions from its target users.

Universal Serial Bus (USB): A standard interface that allows peripheral devices (digital cameras, printers, MP3 players, game joysticks, keyboards, mice, etc.) to be attached to computers. The majority of thumb drives connect to computers via a USB port.

User Datagram Protocol (UDP): A part of the IP (Internet Protocol) suite of protocols. UDP is known as a connectionless protocol, since it does not perform any checking to ensure that the receiving computer gets all data that it is supposed to. By not performing such checking, UDP is much quicker than TCP is. A common use of UDP is for streaming audio over the Internet. The skips heard in the music are examples of dropped data packets. The lack of error checking makes UDP inappropriate for use where receipt of all data sent is critical.

Virtual Private Network (VPN): A secure and private communications channel companies use to communicate with each other over a public network such as the Internet. Virtual Private Networks also allow remote users to securely connect to their company's network. VPNs are generally protected by both a username/password as well as a separate form of authentication such as an ID/fob (Token).

Virus: A computer virus is a malicious software program that has the ability to replicate itself and to infect a computer with neither the knowledge nor the permission of the end-user. The original virus is capable of making modified copies of itself, and the copies may also make changes to themselves, as is the case with what is known as a metamorphic virus. This is similar to how the flu virus that affects humans changes from year to year. A computer virus cannot spread from computer to computer by itself, but requires a delivery method to attack uninfected computers. However, this can be accomplished in many different ways. An end-user can unknowingly send a computer virus to others in the form of an e-mail. Computer viruses can also be spread by sharing data on removable devices such as CDs or thumb drives. Since many computers are now connected to the Internet, computer viruses can spread to a great number of systems quite quickly. Not only can a computer virus reproduce itself, but its copies can reproduce as well. In this way, their growth can be exponential in nature. Some computer viruses are malicious in nature and can damage programs, delete files, and even format computer hard drives. Other viruses are more of a nuisance, and often reveal themselves as a "harmless" video or audio message. Even the more benign computer viruses can cause problems in the form of performance degradation. Today, there are quite literally millions of computer viruses in existence, with new ones being discovered daily.

Warm Site: A backup facility that has a higher degree of readiness than a cold site does, but less than a hot site. A warm site generally consists of many, but not all, of the components that a company will need to use in the event of an emergency.

Webmail: Internet (Web) based e-mail, which is in contrast to desktop-based e-mail clients such as Microsoft Outlook. Common Web mail implementations include Hotmail, Yahoo Mail, Gmail, and more. They are generally free of charge for anybody who has Internet access.

Wi-Fi Protected Access (WPA-2): A method used to encrypt data as it is being transmitted over wireless computer networks. It is the current de facto standard protocol for securely sending data over wireless networks. WPA-2 was developed when weaknesses were discovered in Wireless Equivalent Protocol (WEP). WPA-2 uses the Advanced Encryption Standard (AES) to encrypt data, versus RC4, used by both WEP and WPA.

Wired Equivalent Privacy (WEP): One of the first standards for protecting data being transmitted over a wireless network. Vulnerabilities discovered in WEP led to it being replaced by WPA and WPA-2 back in the 2003 and 2004, respectively. Using readily available software tools, WEP can be cracked in less than one minute. For that reason, it is no longer appropriate for use in sending sensitive data over wireless networks.

Worms: A program that is self-replicating. A computer worm is also capable of sending itself to other computers on a network without any manual human intervention. Worms can cause damage by design, and if nothing else can take up network bandwidth as they send themselves to other systems on the network. Unlike a virus, a computer worm does not need to attach itself to another program.

Zombie Computer: A computer that has been compromised by a hacker unbeknownst to its legitimate user. A "zombied" computer will function normally. It will carry out the intent of the hacker when given further instructions remotely, or at a predetermined time based on instructions included at the time the computer was compromised. Hackers generally create zombies both to hide their true identities and also to increase their attack power by taking over a large number of computers.

INDEX

Access Control List, 33, 141, 147, 161
Administrator Account, 161
Adware, 87-88, 161
The Americans with Disabilities Act
    (ADA), 96, 100
Analog or analogue, 30, 32, 65, 161
Anonymous FTP, 38, 161
Anti-virus, 3, 10, 25, 31, 60, 84, 86, 88
AS400, 21, 170
Asymmetric Cryptography, 106, 161
Audit, 13, 17, 19, 31, 33, 35, 37, 43,
    49-50, 56, 63, 73, 103, 116, 130-31,
    133, 142-43, 145
Authentication, 12, 18, 22-23, 35, 44-
    45, 50-60, 62-63, 65-66, 106, 143, 146
Authorization, 49-51, 59-60, 63, 141-42

Back Door, 6, 170
Bastion Host, 22-23, 162
Bluejacking, 69, 162
Bluesnarfing, 69, 162
Bluetooth, 69, 162
Bollard, 48, 162
The British Standards Institute (BSI),
    73, 103, 160, 162,
Brute force attack, 57, 162
Business Continuity Planning (BCP),
    71, 73-81, 162

The Civil Contingencies Act 2004, 73
Client/Server Applications, 62, 162
Code Red, 86
Cold Site, 75, 163, 170
Concurrent Versions System (CVS),
    26

Contracts, 48, 115, 118, 120, 135
Cookies, 87, 88, 163
Cryptography, 62, 161, 162

Degaussing, 120, 163
Demilitarized Zone, 20-21, 163
Denial-of-Service Attack (DoS attack),
    119, 163
Development Environment, 2, 6, 24,
    25, 163, 166
Dictionary attack, 57, 163
Digital, 65, 150, 161, 163, 167, 169
Disclosure, 4, 14, 18, 21, 39, 115-16,
    123-28, 134-135
Dynamic Host Configuration
    Protocol (DHCP), 28, 163-64

Encryption, 10-14, 22-23, 28-29, 31,
    36-38, 45, 51-52, 62, 65-67, 70, 106,
    117, 123-24, 136, 164-67
Exploits, 6-7, 34, 164
Extranet, 21, 164

Federal Educational Rights and
    Privacy Act (FERPA), 130-131
Financial Institution Shared
    Assessment Program (FISAP), 116
Firecall ID, 27, 164
Firewall, 5, 7, 11-12, 20-21, 23, 29-37,
    39, 60, 65, 82, 87, 89, 102, 106, 138,
    162-65, 167-68
Firewall Rules, 7, 32, 33, 164
FTP, 22, 38, 161, 164, 168
FTPS (Commonly referred to as
    FTP/SSL), 38, 164, 168

Gigabyte, 9, 89, 164, 169
Gramm-Leach-Bliley Act (GLBA), 129-30
Graphical user interface (GUI), 84, 164

Hacker, 6-7, 10, 20-21, 23, 28, 30, 32-34, 37, 38, 44-45, 49, 51-52, 54-55, 58, 59, 63, 65, 66, 69, 80, 82-85, 88, 89, 91-92, 94-95, 105, 118, 124, 138, 164-65
Hashing, 22, 165
The Health Insurance Portability and Accountability Act (HIPAA), 14-15, 130
Hot fix, 22, 165
Hot Site, 75, 165
HTTP, 165
HTPS, 38, 165
Hub, 76, 165

ID/Fob, 27, 52, 56, 58, 61, 66, 165
Internet Control Message Protocol (ICMP), 34
Intrusion Detection Sensor (IDS), 35, 36, 66, 165
Intrusion Prevention Sensor (IPS), 36, 165
IP Spoofing, 28, 174
Information Technology Security Evaluation Criteria (ITSEC), 15

JPEG, 2, 166

Kerberos, 62-63, 166

Media Access Control address (MAC address), 28, 54, 166
Maintenance Hooks, 65, 166
Malware, 2, 86-87, 166
Master Image File, 9, 166
Megabit, 136, 166
Megabyte, 89, 166
Modems, 9, 27, 37, 64-66, 136
MS-DOS (Microsoft Disk Operating System), 89, 166
Multicast Traffic, 32

Network address translation (NAT), 33, 167
Network File System (NFS), 34
Nimda, 87

Patch, 7, 10, 16, 22, 25, 38, 76, 84, 86, 89, 114, 143, 167
The Payment Card Industry Data Security Standard (PCI), 14, 130
Ping, 34, 167
Pretty Good Privacy (PGP), 45, 167
Production System, 2, 6-7, 24-25, 140, 167
Protocol, 32, 34, 34, 37, 110, 167
Proxy-based Firewall, 32, 167
Public Key Infrastructure (PKI), 45, 167

Remote Procedure Call (PRC), 32, 34, 167
Removable Media Encryption (RME), 67, 167
Root, 60, 167
Router, 10, 12, 23, 33-35, 38, 76-77, 167

Sally port, 46, 53, 168
Sarbanes-Oxley (SOX), 41, 130,
Secret-Key Cryptography, 62, 168
Secure Shell (SSH), 37, 38, 110, 168
Secure Socket Layer (SSL), 38, 110, 168
Stateful Inspection Firewall, 32-33, 168
Statement on Auditing Standards No. 70 (SAS 70), 116
SFTP, 38, 168
S/MIME, 45, 166
Spyware, 87, 88, 168
Switch, 76-77, 103, 136, 168
Symmetric cryptography, 62, 106

T1 line, 136, 169
Trusted Computer System Evaluation Criteria (TCSEC), 15-16, 38, 141, 145-47, 169
Terabyte, 89, 169
Traceroute, 34, 169
Trojan horse, 2, 86, 169

Universal Serial Bus (USB), 9-0, 169

Virtual Private Network (VPN), 27, 29, 37, 64, 66-67, 74, 79, 170
Virus, 2, 20, 72, 86-89, 119, 170

War Games, 65

Warm Site, 75, 170
Web mail, 2, 57, 170
Wi-Fi Protected Access (WPA-2), 28, 170
Worms, 86, 170

Zombie computer, 44, 171

ABOUT THE AUTHOR

PHILIP ALEXANDER began his career in computers back in the late 1980s while serving in the U.S. military. Since then, he has worked in both the public and private sectors in positions including engineer, project manager, principal security consultant, security architect, and information technology director. He currently works for a major financial institution as an information security officer.

Phil is also an avid public speaker, and regularly presents at security conferences around the country and abroad on a wide range of topics. He has published a number of information security articles as well. This is the second book that he has published. The first book is titled *Data Breach Disclosure Laws: A State By State Perspective*, which was published in March 2007. The book documents the data breach laws of the more than 35 states that have such laws within the United States.